THE UNDERESTIMATED GOSPEL

TOGETHER FOR
THE GOSPEL

THE UNDERESTIMATED GOSPEL

R. Albert **MOHLER** Jr.
Thabiti **ANYABWILE**
David **PLATT**
Kevin **DEYOUNG**
Mark **DEVER**
C.J. **MAHANEY**
Matt **CHANDLER**
John **PIPER**
J. Ligon **DUNCAN** III

Jonathan Leeman – General Editor

B&H
PUBLISHING GROUP
Nashville, Tennessee

978-1-4336-8390-9

Published by B&H Publishing Group

Nashville, Tennessee

Dewey Decimal Classification: 226

Subject Heading: BIBLE. N.T. GOSPELS \
CHRISTIAN LIFE \ GOSPEL

1 2 3 4 5 6 7 8 9 • 18 17 16 15 14

CONTENTS

The Power of the Gospel

Power for the Church

FOREWORD

Matt Schmucker

For Mark Dever's pastoral installation service at Capitol Hill Baptist Church in September 1994, a neighboring church's pastor was asked to participate. He welcomed Mark to the Capitol Hill neighborhood by referring to "my good friend Mark Dever," but he pronounced Mark's last name "Deaver" as in beaver, rather than Dever as in never.

Good friend? Really?

That week marked my tenth anniversary of being a Christian, and I cannot say I had been encouraged by what I had seen of church leaders in those ten years. Mostly I had encountered the clubby, partisan, institution-bound individuals who lived by the creed "Go along to get along." Or I had run across the strongly dogmatic characters who have biting and condescending words for any fellow Christians who disagreed with them. Needless to say, I wasn't impressed with either group; and certainly I was not impressed with the pretense of friendship when there is none.

This is why I love Together for the Gospel (T4G). The men behind this conference—and the authors of this book—have a real and deep knowledge of and affection for each other. Even more impressive, they have a real and deep unity despite the myriad issues that have separated other men. Back in 2006 at the first T4G conference Mark Dever's introductory comments included this about his fellow speakers:

> We wouldn't agree on any number of matters. We
> didn't even agree on what to wear, or what kind
> of pulpit to use. We barely got agreement on the
> music. Our music is not all alike, nor are we simi
> larly expressive in singing. Our introductions would
> be different. Some would respond to a sermon with
> applause, others would say "Amen" (and even that we
> would pronounce differently!). But, it was for none
> of these reasons that we come together. We come
> together for what we do agree on; we come together
> for the gospel.

Al Mohler put it succinctly when he said, "I have more in common with a thick Presbyterian than I do with a thin Baptist." He and Ligon Duncan, a "thick" Presbyterian, share far more in common than either do with someone in their own denominations who don't affirm the inerrancy of Scripture, the resurrection, or the virgin birth.

Has their friendship been tested? I grew up with six brothers. I know brothers can fight. These guys fight and argue like everyone else. (I've found myself dazed and confused many times sitting in their meetings watching the great theological debates of the day flash before my eyes.) But what I've seen from them is that the gospel is thicker than blood. Unity prevails! Some of these men have endured great physical challenges, others blistering public scrutiny such that you'd rather have the skin ripped off your back. Yet they stood—together. Job could have used friends like these.

In Philippians 2:2, Paul told the Philippians to "make my joy complete by being like-minded, having the same love, being one in spirit and purpose" (NIV 1984). I have seen this call beautifully modeled in how these brothers, preachers, and authors differ with one another in eschatology and ecclesiology.

How do I know? I have had the privilege of a lifetime to work with these men to help organize T4G 2006, 2008, 2010, and 2012. We have met many times. I'm happy to call all of them "Pastor." Therefore, with full confidence I commend both the messages of this book and the men behind them. More important, I join with these brothers and commend Jesus Christ who is the gospel and the only reason we are *together*.

> "How good and pleasant it is when brothers live
> together in unity!" (Ps. 133:1 NIV 1984)

INTRODUCTION

Jonathan Leeman

If you have not read Arnold Dallimore's two-volume biography of George Whitefield, you might consider taking the first volume on your next vacation. It is both edifying and enjoyable, but you will need more than one vacation to get through both tomes.

The book offers a remarkable chronicle of "the life and times of the great evangelist of the eighteenth-century revival," as the subtitle has it. Interestingly, it opens by describing the moral corruption and spiritual decay that characterized post-Puritan England in the early eighteenth century, the kind of declension that caused some to conclude that God was done with England. Maybe you think the same thing about the global West today? Yet into this dark night came a young Anglican minister who preached the justice and mercy of God, the goodness and guilt of humanity, the substitution and resurrection of Christ, and the call to repentance and belief. Unaccommodating clergy forced Whitefield out of their church buildings and into the open fields, where, by God's typically atypical designs, thousands, even tens of thousands, could gather to hear Whitefield's underestimated gospel. And respond. Throughout England and America, conversions numbered in the tens of thousands, if not hundreds of thousands. Historians call it the First Great Awakening.

1

Yet Dallimore did not write as a dispassionate historian. He admits in the introduction that "this book goes forth with a mission." First published in 1970, when the oldest preacher in the volume that you are now holding was a seminary student and the youngest was nine years short of birth, Dallimore hoped the stories of Whitefield would stoke the fires of gospel revival in our own day. And he knew it would take a new generation of preachers to stand squarely on the Scriptures and the gospel. Prophetically, he writes:

> Yet this book is written in the desire—perhaps in a measure of inner certainty—that we shall see the great Head of the Church once more bring into being His special instruments of revival, that He will again raise up unto Himself certain young men whom He may use in this glorious employ. And what manner of men will they be? Men mighty in the Scriptures, their lives dominated by a sense of the greatness, the majesty and holiness of God, and their minds and hearts aglow with the great truths of the doctrines of grace. They will be men who have learned what it is to die to self, to human aims and personal ambitions; men who are willing to be "fools for Christ's sake", who bear reproach and falsehood, who will labour and suffer, and whose supreme desire will be, not to gain earth's accolades, but to win the Master's approbation when they appear before His awesome judgment seat. They will be men who will preach with broken hearts and tear-filled eyes, and upon whose ministries God will grant an extraordinary effusion of the Holy Spirit, and who will witness "signs and wonders following" in the transformation of multitudes of human lives.[1]

The biographer concludes these remarks with the "earnest prayer that, amidst the rampant iniquity and glaring apostasy" of our day, God would raise up a new generation of such men "toward the granting of a mighty revival such as was witnessed two hundred years ago."[2]

Any Christian who stops to consider the matter would surely echo the late Dallimore's prayer. What Christian's heart does not yearn for our neighbors to wake up to the deceitful nature of sin. Sin promises the world, but only provides a two-dimensional cardboard version, like a theater stage set, not to mention the divine wrath to come. And we know that, if only our friends and neighbors would turn and be converted, the full-life, warm-breath embrace of a Creator and Savior awaits. How this embrace has given joy and hope to our own sin-clouded hearts!

Lord God, will you raise up a generation of such preachers? Will your Spirit use them toward the granting of a mighty revival in our day? In our land? Among those whom we know and love? Will you bring not just a few but many conversions?

In April 2012, almost eight thousand church leaders sat for three weekdays in the cramped folding chairs of a college basketball arena in Louisville, Kentucky, to hear the nine sermons and eight testimonies which comprise this volume. Some of us sitting in attendance wondered if the event (and others like it going on these days) represented more evidence of God's answer to Dallimore's prayer. The event was called Together for the Gospel (T4G), which is a biennial pastor's conference that began with the friendship of four preachers in 2006 and has always included several other prominent voices in the movement of reformed evangelical churches.

No one dares assume that any of T4G's speakers will make the multinational, multi-centuries impact of George Whitefield. And the conference itself is aimed not at unconverted plowmen and housewives, lawyers and soldiers, like Whitefield's open-air sermons. It is aimed at converted pastors and other church leaders. In fact, the closest thing to Whitefield today, at least in terms of sheer statistics, would be one of several prosperity preachers whose road show fills stadiums around the globe week after week with tens of thousands of souls desperate for the God of health and wealth to provide them with salvation *and* a bigger house. No, four installments of the T4G conference, including 2012's, gives no ground for triumphalism. It has not visibly led to the salvation of tens of thousands and changed the face of a nation, as God seemed to do through the famed preacher of yesteryear.

But the phenomenon of T4G has produced longing. Deep longing. Revival longing. Imagine standing in a room with eight thousand other people of God, singing the words "In Christ alone my hope is found, he is my light, my strength, my song." Feel the stadium's echo press those voices back onto your chest while the floor beneath your feet vibrates and adrenaline makes your hands tingle. Then sit and listen as some of the finest preachers of our day extol the power of the underestimated gospel, gripping, again, both body and soul.

Might God not do something extraordinary today? God, please? Maybe there is no ten-megaton bomb like Whitefield, but what about placing a single stick of dynamite in eight thousand pairs of hands? What kind of explosion would that make as such gospel proclaimers spread across the face of the nations? It is the Lord's to decide such things, but it is ours to ask and to work. It was not finally Whitefield who was so powerful; it was the gospel that he preached and the Lord that he served. And do we not have Whitefield's gospel and Lord?

The hope of T4G and other like-minded conferences and organizations in the present day is that they would represent not the culmination of revival, but the kindling.

⤌

The sermons that have become chapters in this book have been lightly edited in order to favor a reader instead of a hearer. And they have been reordered in the table of contents to better fit under topical subheadings. But their general sermonic form and voice remains, and the sermons which explicitly addressed the audience as pastors retain that address.

The theme of the 2012 conference was "The Underestimated Gospel." The idea is that the gospel consists merely of words, but those words have the unexpected and underestimated power to create new life, to justify, to prepare a bride, to give the foretaste of glory. Christian conversion depends upon the underestimated power of the gospel.

Such conversions were recounted throughout the course of the 2012 conference. I was a drug dealer. I grew up in a bar. I was raised by Christian parents. I was an illegal immigrant. I was a counselor to a US senator. But God saved me. But God changed me. Don't underestimate the power of the gospel.

These testimonies have been written down and interspersed throughout the chapters of this book. The bulk of the book, of course, are the sermons. T4G began in 2006 with the friendship of Mark Dever, J. Ligon Duncan III, C. J. Mahaney, and R. Albert Mohler Jr., who then invited a marginally older generation of friends: John Piper, R. C. Sproul, and John MacArthur. As the years have passed and the older generation has gradually stepped away, the four friends have turned and begun to invite a younger generation, beginning with Thabiti Anyabwile in 2008, and then Matt Chandler, Kevin DeYoung, and David Platt in 2012.

In this volume, R. Albert Mohler Jr., Thabiti Anyabwile, and David Platt get the ball rolling by reflecting directly upon this powerful gospel. Mohler draws from Romans 10 to argue that gospel must be spoken in words. You cannot know the good news of God in Christ unless someone draws near to you and speaks words. Yes, deeds are a crucial component of Christian witness, but there is no salvation apart from articulated words. Anyabwile turns to 1 Timothy 1:12–17 in order to showcase the conversion of one of the Bible's worst terrorists, the murderous Saul who became the apostle Paul. He then leverages this remarkable example to ask about our own confidence as gospel-believers. Are we putting our confidence in something besides the gospel's power, and do our evangelistic practices demonstrate that we believe God can convert the most unlikely of sinners? Platt picks up on this theme of confidence by looking especially at one aspect of the gospel featured in Revelation 5:1–14, namely, that Christ's atone-ment is "graciously, globally, and gloriously particular." The fact that Christ has graciously died for a global and particular people means that pastors and churches should pray confidently, give sacrificially, go intentionally, and die willingly. Do we?

If the power of conversion and change depend upon God's work through the gospel, how should we understand Christian growth both individually and corporately? This is the question that Kevin DeYoung and Mark Dever undertake to answer. If we are justi-fied through faith, isn't it true that we are also sanctified through faith? Yes, says DeYoung, but "through" means something different. This latter gift from God comes through divinely enabled toil and effort. It is not enough to say, "look to the Lord" or "get gripped by the gospel." Growth in the underestimated gospel requires Spirit-powered, gospel-driven, faith-fueled work. Dever in turn considers how carelessness in our life and doctrine have led to so many false conversions, which, in turn, deceive people about their own salva-tion and undermine the church's witness. So preach the gospel fully and rightly, which includes the promise of God's judgment and the exclusivity of Christ. Don't shape the gospel around consumer preferences, lest your church become a market for consumers who only think they are Christians.

Three more pastors then personally draw from the hard roads of experience to offer gospel-soothing words to weary brothers walking down the same roads. C. J. Mahaney meditates on 2 Corinthians 4 in order to find comfort from Paul's example: "death is at work in us, but life in you." This gospel ministry feels like death, but don't you remember that ministerial death produces life? As with your Savior? We discover the power of the resurrection through the very process of suffering. John Piper flips forward to Jude to ask whether we can measure this underestimated and unaccountable power that saves the believer and then preserves him through life's toils and snares. Piper wonders, do we measure it like pounds of pressure? Or kilowatts of electrical force? Or roentgens of radiation? The answer, you will see from the title of his talk, has to do with the glory, majesty, dominion, and authority of God. Matt Chandler then escorts us into the throne room of Revelation 21 and asks us to cast our eyes around. Yes, the glories and agonies of pastoral ministry, each succeeding the other in rapid succession through the course of a working week, can make the head spin. But great hope can be found by keeping the end in sight. Are you looking?

J. Ligon Duncan III, finally, points to all our good longings— our longings for conversions, for healthy churches, for a new generation of faithful preachers and evangelists, for revival—and he gently takes us by the hand and walks us back to Elijah. He asks us to sit down with Elijah for a moment as Elijah nurses his own wounds and contemplates his pastoral disappointments and failed dreams. How do we respond when God does not give the good things for which we've prayed and yearned and suffered for years of ministry? Could it be that we, somehow, have idolized the good things? And could it be that God is preparing us for an even greater vision to come?

Do not underestimate the gospel, and do not underestimate the God of this gospel.

❧

Everyone is looking for power. Political campaigns play to the power of fear and hope. Advertising agencies rely on the power of appetite.

But churches have something different and better. Churches have the gospel.

Though we live in the world, we must not wage war like the world, or fight with its weapons. On the contrary, we have divine power to demolish strongholds. To declare the forgiveness of sin. To create life. To promise the very transformation of the universe. Talk about power.

Witness the underestimated gospel!

1

THE POWER OF THE ARTICULATED GOSPEL

R. Albert Mohler Jr.

Scripture quotations in this chapter are from ESV.

Even as we are together for the gospel, we want to be certain that we are together for the authentic gospel. There is only one gospel that saves—the gospel of Jesus Christ as revealed in the Scriptures. We want to make certain that we are accountable to that gospel. We do not want to underestimate it or, to use a word coined by former President George W. Bush, we do not want to misunderestimate the gospel. We want all of it, and we need all of it.

When we first came "Together for the Gospel" in 2006, we put forth a written series of "Affirmations and Denials." We began with these words:

> We are brothers in Christ united in one great cause:
> to stand together for the gospel. We are convinced
> that the gospel of Jesus Christ has been misrepre-
> sented, misunderstood and marginalized in many

churches and among many who claim the name of
Christ. Compromise of the gospel has led to the
preaching of false gospels, the seduction of many
minds and movements and the weakening of the
church's gospel witness.[1]

In other words, coming together to be in the gospel means that
we have to know what the gospel *is*, and that also means we have to
be candid about what the gospel is *not*. What was true in 2006 is all
the more the reality today; we are surrounded by misunderstandings
and misconstruals of the gospel.

I must admit something up front. I miss *Calvin and Hobbes*—
and I am referring specifically to the comic strip by that name, not
the theologian and the philosopher. I miss *The Far Side* too. Ever
since these two went into retirement, we are left without anything
quite like them. My daily mirth from the newspaper is not nearly
as mirthy as it was before. I am not a big fan of *Dilbert*, but there
is one that has just stuck in my mind. Dilbert, the office worker
and main character of the comic strip, talks with Dogbert, his little
dog-friend. As the two of them are in conversation, Dilbert spins
out an elaborate theory of the universe. Dogbert listens patiently
all the way to the end, only to say, "That comes so close to being
interesting."

I have heard sermons that I thought came dangerously close to
having a point, dangerously close to actually getting it right—but
did not. As Christians in general, and as ministers of the gospel in
particular, the haunting fear we have is that we will fall short, coming dangerously close to preaching the gospel. That is yet another
reason why we need to talk about the gospel—to make certain we are
saying the right things about the gospel. We must hold one another
accountable to fulfill what Paul said to Timothy: "Follow the pattern
of the sound words" (2 Tim. 1:13)—the gospel of Jesus Christ.

The gospel has enemies, but sometimes it is underestimated even by its friends. In Romans 1:16, Paul said, "For I am not ashamed of the gospel, for it is the power of God for salvation to everyone who believes, to the Jew first and also to the Greek." We preach this gospel because we know it is the power to save; Christ saves! We want to be a gospel people leading gospel churches in a great global gospel movement. We long to see the renown of Jesus and his salvation known among every tribe and people and nation (Rev. 5:9). We want to live gospel lives filled with gospel evidences and gracious signs of the gospel. We want to know the joy of the gospel, bear the fruit of the gospel, and see gospel people set loose in the world. And, as we do so, we must realize the very real danger that we can underestimate the gospel—even as we think and say we love it.

Within the previously mentioned "Together for the Gospel: Affirmations and Denials" adopted in 2006, we made these statements about the gospel:

> **Article VIII:** We affirm that salvation is all of grace and that the gospel is revealed to us in doctrines that most faithfully exalt God's sovereign purpose to save sinners and in His determination to save His redeemed people by grace alone through faith alone in Christ alone to His glory alone.
>
> We deny that any teaching, theological system or means of presenting the gospel that denies the centrality of God's grace as His gift of unmerited favor to sinners in Christ can be considered true doctrine.
>
> **Article IX:** We affirm that the gospel of Jesus Christ is God's means of bringing salvation to His people, that sinners are commanded to believe the gospel and that the church is commissioned to preach and teach the gospel to all nations.

We deny that evangelism can be reduced to any program, technique or marketing approach. We further deny that salvation can be separated from repentance toward God and faith in our Lord Jesus Christ.

Article X: We affirm that salvation comes to those who truly believe and confess that Jesus Christ is Lord.

We deny that there is salvation in any other name or that saving faith can take any form other than conscious belief in the Lord Jesus Christ and His saving acts.[2]

Since 2006, not one of these issues has gone away. Furthermore, new complexities, compromises, and temptations have been added. The issues are reframed, but the question remains: Are we really preaching and obeying the whole gospel?

We know that what is called Evangelicalism includes those who see the gospel as nothing more than a transaction or decision that leads to their eternal salvation, with no reference to the lordship of Christ and the command to be his faithful disciple. We know that many churches would say that they love the gospel but are filled with people who do not look like gospel people and seem unaware or unconcerned about that fact.

Over a generation ago, Carl Henry wrote a book, the title of which made clear the problem: *A Plea for Evangelical Demonstration*.[3] Henry's call is rightly being heard anew today by a generation that will not be satisfied until our churches begin to look more like gospel people. This is real and right and necessary. But first, the gospel has to be heard, and for it to be heard it has to be articulated. Therefore, we dare not underestimate the power of the articulated gospel.

Romans 10

The apostle Paul makes clear the necessity and potency of the articulated gospel in the tenth chapter of his letter to the Romans:

> For Moses writes about the righteousness that is based on the law, that the person who does the commandments shall live by them. But the righteousness based on faith says, "Do not say in your heart, 'Who will ascend into heaven?'" (that is, to bring Christ down) "or 'Who will descend into the abyss?'" (that is, to bring Christ up from the dead). But what does it say? "The word is near you, in your mouth and in your heart" (that is, the word of faith that we proclaim); because, if you confess with your mouth that Jesus is Lord and believe in your heart that God raised him from the dead, you will be saved. For with the heart one believes and is justified, and with the mouth one confesses and is saved. For the Scripture says, "Everyone who believes in him will not be put to shame." For there is no distinction between Jew and Greek; for the same Lord is Lord of all, bestowing his riches on all who call on him. For "everyone who calls on the name of the Lord will be saved."
>
> How then will they call on him in whom they have not believed? And how are they to believe in him of whom they have never heard? And how are they to hear without someone preaching? And how are they to preach unless they are sent? As it is written, "How beautiful are the feet of those who preach the good news!" But they have not all obeyed the gospel. For Isaiah says, "Lord, who has believed what he has heard from us?" So faith comes from hearing,

and hearing through the word of Christ. (Rom.
10:5–17)

Paul's great apostolic concern here is the refusal of his kinsmen
to believe in Christ and be saved. Within the context of this section
of Romans, Paul writes about the relationship between the Jewish
people (the people of the old covenant) and believers (the redeemed
in the new covenant). Although a Jew by birth and religious practice,
Paul writes as an apostle of the Lord Jesus Christ to a congregation
consisting of believers who come from both Jewish and Gentile back-
grounds. Paul writes of the priority of God's covenant people and of
the promises that were made to Israel, but he makes the centrality
and the universality of the gospel clear. He makes the universality of
our human need clear in terms of our depravity: "for all have sinned
and fall short of the glory of God" (Rom. 3:23).

Paul demonstrates justification by faith as having been revealed in
the Old Testament when Abraham was declared righteous on the basis
of his faith. Later, we come to understand that it was on the basis of
what Christ had done for Abraham. In Romans, we read how Christ's
atonement fully satisfies both the wrath and the righteousness of God.
We come to understand how God set forth Christ as a propitiation in
his blood such that the Father is now demonstrated to be both the just
and the justifier of the one who has faith in Jesus Christ. As a result,
in Christ there is no condemnation that comes to us (Rom. 8:1). Then,
the apostle Paul writes a chapter which quintessentially displays the
sovereignty of God (Rom. 9), before turning to our present text which
Charles Spurgeon described as "the whole machinery of salvation."[4]
The gospel is all here, and it is all glorious.

The Word Brought Near

First, we see in this text that the Word must be brought near. How did any of us come to know the Lord Jesus Christ as Savior, to have our sins forgiven, and to come to faith in Christ? We are saved because the Word is brought near to us. As the author of the book of Hebrews writes, "Long ago, at many times and in many ways, God spoke to our fathers by the prophets, but in these last days he has spoken to us by his Son" (Heb. 1:1–2). The Word is brought near in revelation, in the promise of the prophets and the Torah, and in every particle of Scripture. Then, the Word is brought near ultimately in Christ, who came near to us and tabernacled with us in his incarnation. Then, the Word is brought near in the apostolic preaching of the gospel.

Then, in verse eight of Romans 10, Paul explains how the Word is brought near to us: "The word is near you, in your mouth and in your heart" (v. 8). Paul quotes Deuteronomy 30:14 to show that the Word was first brought near to Israel. Moses reminded the children of Israel that they did not go to *find* the Torah. No, the Torah was *given* to them. This serves as a helpful reminder that our salvation is all of grace. Just as they were God's elect people, chosen from among the nations, one of the reasons they knew God chose them is because of the testimony of Deuteronomy 4:33: "Did any people ever hear the voice of a god speaking out of the midst of the fire, as you have heard, and still live?" No! The Word was brought near to us and now it is near to us. Life is in obedience and death is in disobedience.

In like manner, the apostle Paul here writes to Jews who now know the gospel of the Lord Jesus Christ because the gospel of Christ was brought near to them. He also writes to Gentiles who have come to know the Lord Jesus Christ as Savior because the Word of the gospel was brought near to them.

The "word being brought near" is a beautiful metaphor of evangelism and of the preaching of the gospel. This is one of the most precious privileges of the Christian life. Proximity to the gospel is not the point; the hearing of the gospel is the point. God brought the Word near to us, and it is our sacred responsibility to bring the Word near to others. For our salvation, the Word was brought near to us in the incarnation of the Lord Jesus Christ and in his saving acts. It is now brought near to sinners through the preaching of the gospel.

Proximity to the gospel is not the point. The hearing of the gospel is the point, and it is by the means of preaching that the gospel is brought near. A Christian may live in close relationship with a person who does not know Christ, but unless the Christian actually articulates the gospel, there is no salvation. The gospel is brought near in verbal form. It is "the word of faith that we proclaim" (Rom. 10:8). This word leads to faith as it articulates the saving acts of Christ and the promise of the gospel. The gospel requires this articulation so that the one who hears it may believe, confess, and be saved.

Paul's apostolic ministry was centered on bringing the Word near to others. He commissioned preachers who would take the Word and preach it in order to bring it near. Paul envisioned all Christians to be evangelists, agents of bringing the saving Word of the gospel near. Therefore, our task is to bring the Word near to others even as it was brought near to us.

The Power of the Gospel to Save

Second, we need to see in this text the power of the gospel to save. This is where we rightly refer to the "well-meant offer of the gospel." We believe that we are to preach the gospel to all persons everywhere, in the firm and unshakable conviction that if they believe and confess, then they will be saved. Paul speaks clearly to this in verses 9–13:

> If you confess with your mouth that Jesus is Lord
> and believe in your heart that God raised him from
> the dead, you will be saved. For with the heart
> one believes and is justified, and with the mouth
> one confesses and is saved. For the Scripture says,
> "Everyone who believes in him will not be put to
> shame." For there is no distinction between Jew and
> Greek; for the same Lord is Lord of all, bestowing
> his riches on all who call on him. For "everyone who
> calls on the name of the Lord will be saved."

There is no footnote or asterisk attached to this verse. There is no conditionality. This is not a hypothetical statement about the power of the gospel. It is an actual, biblical, apostolic, revealed, inerrant, infallible promise: if sinners believe and confess, they will be saved. That is the well-meant offer of the gospel. We don't present the gospel with one hand behind our back, thinking about the person to whom we are speaking, "This *might* be for you . . . or it might *not* be for you." We don't find refuge in the sovereignty of God in order to say that we don't have to preach the gospel to all persons.

The same Paul who, in chapters eight through nine wrote so clearly about our salvation in terms of God's absolute sovereignty, foreknowledge, predestination, calling and election leading to justification and glorification, now also affirms without qualification that "everyone who calls on the name of the Lord will be saved."

How do we know the elect? It is because they believe and they confess and they are saved—and that requires the means of the preaching of the gospel. Gospel people believe this, live this, and teach this: "Everyone who calls on the name of the Lord will be saved."

What does it mean to call upon the name of the Lord? The answer to that is found in verse nine. Calling on the name of the

Lord means you "confess with your mouth that Jesus Christ is Lord and believe in your heart that God raised him from the dead."

Verse eleven would lead us to be promiscuous and undiscriminating in our preaching of the gospel: "Everyone who believes in him will not be put to shame." Jesus' sower of the seed in the parable of the soils provides confidence and encouragement for us in this work. We are to sow the seed, and we are to do so indiscriminately. We are not in the soil sampling business; we're not in the soil management business; we are in the sowing business. We are told that the harvest will be so magnificent that the sowing of the seed of the gospel will produce believers from every tongue and tribe and people and nation. God bless those evangelists, preachers, teachers, and believers who just keep at it—sowing and sowing and sowing—when they don't even get to see any harvest. They are not confident in their own power to witness, but they are confident in the power of the gospel to save.

Central to all of this is our understanding of the necessity of personal confession, the evidence of personal faith and belief that produces repentance: "For with the heart one believes and is justified, and with the mouth one confesses and is saved" (Rom. 10:10). The death and resurrection of the Lord Jesus Christ are indeed the saving acts of God that are declared in the gospel. We believe that election to salvation and the transforming power of the gospel become evident in faith and repentance and in confession.

Then, in verse twelve, we encounter the revolutionary statement, "there is no distinction between Jew and Greek." Paul, writing to a church experiencing division between those with a Jewish and those with a Gentile background, teaches that at the cross there is no distinction. In terms of our need for a Savior and the Savior's provision, there is no distinction. "Everyone who calls on the name of the Lord will be saved." This hearkens back to the opening of Paul's letter: "For I am not ashamed of the gospel, for it is the power of God for salvation to everyone who believes, to the Jew first and also to the Greek" (Rom. 1:16). That includes all of us; there is no distinction.

This explains why we are saved. In the mystery of the sovereign purposes of God and by his sheer grace and mercy alone, the Word was brought near to us. As a result, we were called, made alive, and regenerated. We then believed what we otherwise would never have been able to believe, and we grasped hold of it, knowing that it is the sole provision of our need. We came to know of our need and of God's response and provision for us in Christ, and then we came to know of our necessary response of faith, repentance, confession, and belief.

The Necessity of Articulating the Gospel

Third, we see in this text the necessity of articulating the gospel. Although our ministry is multidimensional and multiphasic, it is most important and essentially verbal. God calls preachers to preach. In order for the gospel to be either received or rejected, it must first be heard, and that requires words. The power of the gospel is that God uses words that, when rightly bearing witness to the saving acts of Christ and to the promise of God in Christ, bring sinners to believe and to be saved.

It has become popular these days to quote Francis of Assisi as saying, "Preach the gospel at all times. Use words if necessary." By way of a historical footnote, these words were probably not said by Francis. There is no reference to this phrase in this form until about two hundred years after his death. I will admit, however, that the quote does sound like something Francis would say. It certainly sounds like all those who would like to believe we can bring the gospel near just by being close to people, or by acting kind, just, righteous, or loving. The reality, however, is that even as we are called to be all of those things—recognizing them to be signs of the gospel—the gospel nonetheless requires articulation. The gospel requires words.

To be clear, we don't want to turn the Francis quote on its head. We don't want to suggest that Christians should be satisfied with a verbal witness to the gospel that is not backed up with the evidences and signs of the gospel. We shouldn't expect to have credibility in preaching the gospel if we are satisfied in not looking like gospel people. We must show evidence of the gospel by our actions and our deeds. However, though the church must demonstrate the gospel with deeds, we cannot evangelize or preach the gospel without words.

The majority of what we do that is most important in life is dependent on words. Think about any major or formative experience in your life, and try to imagine that event happening without words. For example, you might be able to *insinuate* a marriage proposal to your beloved, but if I may give a suggestion to single men: use words!

The fact is, part of what it means to be made in God's image is that we use words. God is a speaking God and we are a speaking people. Words are essential to our understanding of who we are, what life means, and most important, what the gospel is.

Walter Ong, one of the great scholars of orality in the twentieth century, argued that virtually all language originates in speech, and only later does it take written form.[5] That is to say, speech is verbal in a way that distinguishes human beings from any other creature. As Ong makes clear, meaning requires orality—the expression of words.

In many churches, the words of the Scripture and the sermon are provided to those who are hearing disabled, by means of American Sign Language. But these are not mere gestures, for the signs are a clear communication of words.

Linguists such as Noam Chomsky and others say that central to what it means to be human is the use of embedded linguistic units—otherwise known as gestures. Some scholars spend a lifetime studying human gestures, and from this study they have come to the conclusion that gestures can be effective in two ways. First, gestures aid in the basic communication of affirmation or denial. Every culture has a basic gesture for "yes" and for "no." Second, gestures are fairly adept at communicating emotional states. Beyond that, however, gestures don't actually do much and, in fact, often bring confusion rather than clarity. That is why Duane Litfin, former president of Wheaton College, argues for the priority of the word over the limitations of gesture.[6]

A friend told me a story that illustrates the limitations of gestures. He pastored a large church, and one Sunday as he was preaching, one of his members suffered a heart attack. A physician in the audience attended to him as several men carried him out the back and closed the door. The congregation, slightly traumatized by the emergency, stopped the service and prayed for the man.

Then, the doctor slipped through the back door and made a hand gesture to the pastor—a gesture also observed by all the members of the large choir sitting behind the pulpit. The pastor read the gesture as meaning, "He's fine," but the choir understood the doctor to be saying, "He's dead."

The pastor proceeded to preach. He preached his full sermon— the entire exposition he had prepared. He held nothing back.

After the service, he met up with his wife and knew something was wrong by the look on her face. "You are one of the most self-centered, arrogant, job-focused men on the planet," she declared.

"What did I do?" he asked.

"A doctor came into your church to tell you that one of your members just died, and you just carried on with your sermon without skipping a beat!" she said.

My friend said, "Wait! You mean, he died?"

He went running down the hall until he found the doctor and asked, "What does *this* mean?"—making the hand gesture the doctor had used.

The doctor reassured him that the sign meant, "He's fine. The man had not died."

The pastor said, "Well, next time please use a different gesture because I have an entire choir, and wife, angry with me because they think your gesture meant he was dead."

It turns out that gestures can get extremely confusing. "Yes" and "no" aren't as clear as they were thought to be.

In contrast, here is the clear indictment of Scripture: we are dead in our trespasses and sin (Eph. 2:1, 5; Col. 2:13). Without words, we remain in our trespasses, but as we hear the pattern of right words and believe and confess that Jesus Christ is Lord, we are saved.

In 1 Thessalonians 2:13, the apostle Paul writes a beautiful summary of evangelism and of the preaching of the gospel:

> And we also thank God constantly for this, that
> when you received the word of God, which you
> heard from us, you accepted it not as the word of
> men but as what it really is, the word of God, which
> is at work in you believers.

Paul tells the Corinthians, "You received the word of God," and then explains how it is that they received it: "you heard from us." They heard the word, then they accepted it as the Word of God.

We only use the words that are available to us—that is, human words. But when those human words rightly represent and present the gospel of the Lord Jesus Christ, they are not heard as merely human words; they are heard as the Word of God, which is at work within believers.

In 1 Corinthians 15:1–11, Paul writes:

> Now I would remind you, brothers, of the gospel
> I preached to you, which you received, in which
> you stand, and by which you are being saved, if you
> hold fast to the word I preached to you—unless you
> believed in vain.
>
> For I delivered to you as of first importance
> what I also received: that Christ died for our sins in
> accordance with the Scriptures, that he was buried,
> that he was raised on the third day in accordance
> with the Scriptures, and that he appeared to Cephas,
> then to the twelve. Then he appeared to more than
> five hundred brothers at one time, most of whom are
> still alive, though some have fallen asleep. Then he
> appeared to James, then to all the apostles. Last of all,
> as to one untimely born, he appeared also to me. For
> I am the least of the apostles, unworthy to be called
> an apostle, because I persecuted the church of God.
> But by the grace of God I am what I am, and his
> grace toward me was not in vain. On the contrary, I
> worked harder than any of them, though it was not I,
> but the grace of God that is with me. Whether then
> it was I or they, so we preach and so you believed.

Note the importance of the word "so" in verse eleven: "*So* we preach and *so* you believed." Without the preaching, there is no believing. In terms of our assignment and the gospel's promise, Paul's logic is airtight: "Faith comes from hearing, and hearing through the word of Christ" (Rom. 10:17). The hearing requires the telling; the telling requires words. Faith comes by hearing; it doesn't come by any other means.

Now, just to clarify, we are not talking about merely the auditory experience of hearing the gospel—the outward call. We know that salvation comes to those who also receive the effectual calling of the

Holy Spirit—the inward call. We understand exactly what Martin
Luther said to his pastoral students:

> His word should do the work alone, without our
> work. Why? Because it is not in my power to fashion
> the hearts of men as the potter moulds the clay, and
> to do with them as I please. I can get no farther than
> to men's ear; their hearts I cannot reach. And since
> I cannot pour faith into their hearts, I cannot, nor
> should I, force any one to have faith. This is God's
> work alone, who causes faith to live in the heart. . . .
> We should preach the Word, but the consequences
> must be left to God's own good pleasure.[7]

This is not something that happened *to* the gospel; the gospel is
not entrapped. Our sovereign God did not present the gospel of the
Lord Jesus Christ, only to now be dissatisfied and frustrated that it
has to be communicated in words. From the start, he intended it to
be communicated. He demonstrates the power of the gospel in the
fact that words—even human words—take on the saving authority
of his own Word as the word of faith, which produces faith and belief
and confession. Therefore, we are not to be ashamed or reluctant to
understand that we are to use words to persuade and to contend.

Some people remove the threat of this problem by taking refuge
in universalism or inclusivism. Others simply deny the existence of
hell and eternal judgment. Still others believe in the idea of "anonymous Christians" or the like. But none of these options are available
to the one who seeks to maintain fidelity to the gospel of Jesus Christ.

I am unapologetically a conversionist. Paul clearly believed that
the transformation of the gospel brings us from one state and status
to another that is radically different. In John 6:63, we read, "It is
the Spirit who gives life; the flesh is no help at all." Our Savior told
Nicodemus, "That which is born of the flesh is flesh, and that which

is born of the Spirit is spirit. Do not marvel that I said to you, 'You must be born again'" (John 3:6–7). And this clear statement on the necessity of the Holy Spirit and the new birth comes just before the equally clear promise "that whoever believes in him should not perish but have eternal life" (John 3:16).

When you put all of that together with Romans 10, you come to understand the unbreakable logic of Paul's argument. How do we expect anyone will believe and be saved if they do not hear? And how are they going to hear if the gospel is never proclaimed? And how will the preaching take place if no one is sent? Although this text is a natural place to turn when commissioning missionaries to their field of service, within its context, the logic of Romans 10 is the entire mechanism of salvation. It is God's plan for how the gospel is to be preached, how sinners are to be reached, and how the name of Jesus is to be made famous among the nations. How will they believe if they never hear? How will they hear without a preacher? Lean into those questions and you will feel the weight of the call for all Christians to take the gospel—the articulated gospel—to all people.

When faithful, we have always known this. As evangelicals, we named ourselves as those who believe in the gospel. We are supposed to be the gospel people. We believe in the authority of the gospel, the life-transforming power of the gospel, and the articulation of the gospel. Furthermore, when we have been at our best and most faithful, we have always said this to one another. Only in fairly recent years have we heard such things as, "Stop talking and show me the gospel." Well, we do need to show the gospel, but what we are really showing is the power and the effect of the gospel. But for the gospel to be heard and believed, it must be articulated.

Evangelicals met together in 1966 for The Berlin World Congress on Evangelism. At that Congress, a definition of evangelism was adopted that quintessentially expressed the necessity for gospel articulation. The statement said:

> Evangelism is the proclamation of the gospel of the
> crucified and risen Christ, the only Redeemer of
> men, according to the Scriptures, with the purpose
> of persuading condemned and lost sinners to put
> their faith in God by receiving and accepting Christ
> as Savior through the power of the Holy Spirit and
> to serve Christ as Lord in every calling of life and
> fellowship of His church, looking toward the Day of
> His coming in glory.[8]

That definition is saturated with Scripture; it is consistent with Scripture. More could be said, but I dare say nothing less can be said. Interestingly enough, this 1966 statement was adopted by evangelicals in order to respond to a 1918 statement which had been adopted by the World Council of Churches. The evangelicals meeting in Berlin in 1966 said that the statement from the 1918 World Council of Churches was not saying enough about the gospel. The statement of 1918 came dangerously close to the gospel of Jesus Christ, but it was not the gospel. The gospel requires exclusivity and the gospel requires confession.

In the preparation for the first Lausanne Conference in 1974, John Stott said,

> Evangelism then is sharing this gospel with others.
> The Good News is Jesus and the good news about
> Jesus that we announce is that He died for our sins
> and was raised from death by the Father, according
> to the Scriptures of the Old and the New Testa-
> ments. And then on the basis of His death and
> resurrection, He offers forgiveness of sins and the
> gift of the Spirit to all those who repent, believe and
> are baptized.[9]

Those evangelicals at Lausanne, meeting under the theme, "The Whole Gospel for the Whole World," adopted a covenant which stated:

> Evangelism itself is the proclamation of the histor-
> ical, biblical Christ as Savior and Lord with a view
> to persuading people to come to Him personally and
> so be reconciled to God.[10]

Most recently, the Lausanne Movement meeting in 2010 in Cape Town, South Africa, produced the "Cape Town Commitment," which affirmed, "The gospel is not a concept that needs fresh ideas, but a story that needs fresh telling."[11] It has to be told. It requires words.

I agree with Christopher Wright when he summarizes the gospel in six points. The gospel is:

1. a Christ-centered story to be told
2. a hope-filled message to be proclaimed
3. a revealed truth to be defended
4. a new status to be received
5. a transformed life to be lived
6. a divine power to be celebrated.[12]

Notice that the first three of these all require words. In order to get to the demonstration of the power of the gospel (points four through six), you first have to have a Christ-centered story to be told, a hope-filled message to be proclaimed, and a revealed truth to be defended. If we are left without words, we cannot fulfill the commission and command of Christ, for we cannot articulate the gospel without words.

We live in a world confused and enticed by false gods and false gospels. The only means of reaching people with the saving gospel of Christ is the articulation of that saving message in words. "Faith comes from hearing, and hearing through the word of Christ" (Rom. 10:17).

Faith without works is dead. We know this is true. We long to see more evidence of the gospel in our churches and in our lives. I certainly long to see more of the fruit of the gospel in my own life. I know that our faith is to be demonstrated, not merely declared. Together, we must learn to be more faithful in demonstration so that the world may see our good works and glorify our Father who is in heaven (Matt. 5:16).

But salvation will not come until the gospel is articulated—complete with the account of our need, God's provision, and our response. We must use words to tell the sacrificial and substitutionary death of Christ on the cross and the power of his resurrection from the dead. We must use words to contend for this gospel and to distinguish it from all false gospels. As John Piper has rightly said on many occasions, "We are the people who have to be willing to die for sentences." I will press that even further to say that we have to be willing to die for words. We cannot preach or teach, nor tell the gospel without words.

The pattern of right words reminds us of our responsibility to get the gospel right. We never want to underestimate the power of the articulated gospel.

Ask yourself this question: How is it that you came to believe? How is it that the gospel came to you? We can think of various ways in which the providence of God, who is so rich in mercy toward us, has been demonstrated to us and how the Word was brought near to us. We can think of a preacher we sat in front of or, amazingly enough, a preacher that was simply seen and heard by means of the Internet, television, or the radio. Sometimes we are surprised to hear that the gospel articulated, even if by means of those technologies, saves. But we should not be.

Sometimes it is someone in a hotel room who, in a moment of desperation, opens a drawer and finds a Gideon's Bible. They open that Bible and the convicting power of the Word leads them to faith and repentance.

Sometimes the opportunity to articulate the gospel comes in one of those completely unexpected and unpredictable providential moments when you are sitting next to someone and you have the opportunity to give an answer for the hope that is in you. The individual to whom you are speaking says, "I believe." You say, "You do?" Why is it that we can be so surprised?

Some of us were raised by Christian parents in a Christian home, and the Word was brought near to us by means of our childhood and the wonderful ministry of the church and the means of grace therein. Even surrounded by all of this, at some point we know the gospel had to be articulated, heard, and believed. These words produced belief in us by means of the mysterious, saving purposes of God.

Pastors, when you get up to preach, your absolute confidence is that—insofar as your words are that pattern of sound words, insofar as they are scriptural, insofar as they are true, insofar as they are gospel-centered, insofar as they present the saving acts of God for us in Christ and call sinners to believe and to repent and to confess—you can take confidence that this is the very means whereby God redeems and saves. Through the articulation of the gospel, God brings persons to faith in the Lord Jesus Christ that they may be forgiven of their sins and receive the gift of life everlasting.

Preaching and articulation are the gospel means of a gracious God who, from before the foundation of the world, desired that his gospel would be proclaimed to the nations by his redeemed people who use words.

So use them. Use the right ones. Never underestimate the power of the articulated gospel.

Go tell it on the mountain,
over the hills and everywhere.
Go tell it on the mountain,
that Jesus Christ is Lord.[13]

Testimony: Mez McConnell

My name is Mez McConnell. My mother ran away with the best man in my parents' wedding. My father was an alcoholic and a gambler who abandoned me and my disabled sister. I was left to the streets at age two, and then lived in foster and children's homes until my teens. I was back on the streets when I was sixteen and in prison at twenty-one, and I was a drug addict for six years.

A group of young men from a local church presented me with the gospel when I was living on the streets. They started playing football in our area and told us about the Lord. At the time I was dealing drugs outside a community center. They talked about my sin and God's wrath. I kicked against it.

Later, men came to see me in prison. Once out of prison, they gave me a place to live. Their witness was critical, but the moment of conversion came when reading a Matthew Henry commentary. I realized that I had to take responsibility for my own rebellion against God and not blame it on my terrible childhood. For the first time I believed.

By God's grace, I went back to school and Bible college, and I am now married and have children. I planted a church for street children and prostitutes in Brazil. I recently finished my second plant, and am now looking to train other young men to do likewise in Scotland's poorest housing projects where more than 50 percent of people have no gospel witness.

Praise God for those who brought the Good News to me. Don't underestimate the power of the gospel!

2

CAN YOUR GOSPEL TRANSFORM A TERRORIST?

Thabiti Anyabwile

Unless otherwise noted, Scripture quotations in this chapter are from NIV 1984.

Six years ago I had the privilege of visiting with my good friends Mack Stiles and John Folmar in the United Arab Emirates. I was there for the second of the Christian-Muslim dialogues sponsored by UAE college students and Mack's company. While there, I attended an evangelism conference hosted by John's church, the United Christian Church of Dubai.

I may never forget sitting in the church's meeting hall as the guest evangelist and workshop leader began the meeting. He asked a simple question to get us started: "What do you think is the greatest hindrance to the gospel of Jesus Christ in the Middle East?"

I sat back in my seat, relaxing in the proud assumption that I knew the various answers that could be given to the question. The participants shared their responses: fear, opportunity, persecution, ignorance, the bad witnesses of other Christians, and so on. As people shared, I felt a self-satisfied, "Yeah, I already know that" nod to each comment. The evangelist respectfully wrote each person's response on a flip chart. He affirmed all these responses as good answers.

Then he humbly offered his answer. He suggested that the greatest hindrance to the gospel is the Christian's lack of confidence in the gospel itself. I was stunned. I hadn't thought of that. My mind gradually moved from the proud surprise that I hadn't thought of the answer myself to a dawning realization that I might actually lack this confidence in the gospel myself. In fact, this issue of confidence in the gospel might be the root of other problems I knew I had, like fear of man.

I knew the gospel. I believed the gospel. I would have said the gospel was central to the life of the church. But I felt exposed that day. As I sat listening to the evangelist expound Romans 1:16, it became more and more evident to me that I lacked confidence in the thing I believed and staked my soul upon. Questions flooded my heart: *Thabiti, are there any evident marks to your ministry that reveal a deep unshakeable confidence in the power of the gospel? Can people see that confidence? Is it evident? Is it obvious? Is it clear and compelling? Or do you lack such bold trust in the Good News?*

Since misery loves company, I would like to ask you the same questions. Think of your own life and ministry. Are there any obvious marks, any compelling evidences that certifies to your own soul and to others who observe your ministry that you have a deep unshakeable confidence in the Good News of Jesus Christ?

More specifically, do you have confidence that the gospel of Jesus Christ is enough to transform the people we think are farthest away, with the hardest heart toward the Lord? Or do we underestimate the gospel's ability to transform the worst of sinners?

The title of this sermon refers to "terrorists." Many of us have particular images that flash to mind when we encounter that word. But don't just think of the dominant stereotype. Try to get in mind the person(s) or category of persons that provoke fear in your heart, the person you're tempted to view as unreachable. It could be the Muslim terrorist detonating bombs in civilian marketplaces or the radical Hindu burning down churches. Or it could be the prostitute down the street; the drug dealer in *that* neighborhood; or Uncle Clint, the violent alcoholic. It could be Mrs. Hatcher, your third grade teacher, or Granny Jones who used to kiss you with her hairy mustache. Fix that person in your mind that causes you to shrink back from sharing the gospel or that causes you to think something more is needed in addition to the gospel to reach and convert that person into a new creature. Then ask yourself: *Am I confident—down in my bones with Romans 1:16-styled unashamedness—in the power of the gospel of Jesus Christ to transform this person? Is Romans 1:16 really my boast? Is that boast obvious in my life and ministry?*

My hope for this message is that God would send his Spirit through his Word to exhort you to one basic thing: To rest all your confidence as a gospel preacher or gospel believer on the broad powerful shoulders of God in the gospel. To recline, as it were, on the strength of the gospel and to cultivate deep confidence in the gospel as our central, vital, and sufficient message in this glorious ministry to which the Lord has called us.

To pursue this goal, I would like to make three basic observations from Paul's brief testimony of conversion in 1 Timothy 1:12–17: the great change in one terrorist's life (vv. 12–13); the great cause of his change (vv. 14–16); and the great celebration that results from the gospel (v. 17).

1. The Great Change in One Terrorist's Life (1 Tim. 1:12–13)

The apostle Paul writes to encourage and instruct young Timothy, a protégé and a pastor now serving the church at Ephesus. Paul begins his instruction by calling Timothy to deal with false teaching and false teachers (vv. 3–4). This falsehood is destroying the Christian faith and witness of some (vv. 5–7). There were false teachers leading to false converts. In this case, there were people turning away from the gospel and turning back to the Law. And Paul tells Timothy that this turn from the truth to the Law is not only inappropriate but applied to the wrong audience (vv. 9–10). They were misusing and misapplying the Law. In fact, it was "contrary to the sound doctrine that conforms to the glorious gospel of the blessed God, which [God] entrusted to [Paul]" (vv. 10–11).

When Paul mentions "the glorious gospel of the blessed God" entrusted to him, the mention of the gospel has a certain effect on him. You might think of the effect that hearing a certain song on the radio has on you. If you are like me, you hear the song and you dance in the car saying, "Hey! That's my song!" No matter what you're doing, you are instantly transported back to the time and the frame of mind when the song first became "your song." You remember the person you were. You remember where you have been. "The glorious gospel of the blessed God" rings like a song in Paul's ears, and when he mentions the gospel and considers that he is entrusted with its stewardship, he is transported to a different time and place.

Verses 12–14 break in on the instruction that Paul had been giving Timothy. Verses 12–17 are a testimony wherein Paul gives us a dramatic before-and-after portrait of the apostle's life. It's like those commercials we sometimes see. *Before*, the guy weighed 700 pounds and couldn't get off the couch. Then he started eating only Subway sandwiches. Now, *after* two years of eating teriyaki chicken subs on wheat bread with no mayo, the same guy weighs 175 pounds and does modeling work for Abercrombie & Fitch. That before-and-after picture illustrates for us the radical transformation a Subway sandwich can produce.

The After Picture

But a Subway transformation is nothing compared to the great change that took place in Paul's life. He gives us the "after" picture first in verse 12: "I thank Christ Jesus our Lord, who has given me strength, that he considered me faithful, appointing me to his service." After the transformation, Paul is now a thankful servant of Jesus Christ. He is a steward of the gospel. He has the gospel in his trust, and he is amazed by it. As he puts it in verse 1, he is "an apostle of Christ Jesus by the command of God our Savior and Christ Jesus our hope." Now he is the man God uses to strengthen and confirm the church.

Remarkably—notice in verse 12—he is amazed by the source of his strength. Christ is giving him strength. That realization occurs frequently in Paul's letters. He writes, "I have been crucified with Christ and I no longer live, but Christ lives in me. The life I live in the body, I live by faith in the Son of God, who loved me and gave himself for me" (Gal. 2:20). Also, "We proclaim him, admonishing and teaching everyone with all wisdom, so that we may present everyone perfect in Christ. To this end I labor, struggling with all his energy, which so powerfully works in me" (Col. 1:28–29).

Paul is a Christ-appointed, Christ-empowered, thanks-giving servant of the gospel of God.

The Before Picture

But he was not always the Paul we see here. Notice the word *once* in verse 13. "Even though I was once a blasphemer and a persecutor and a violent man . . ." Paul had a past. He was a blasphemer, someone who opposed and slandered God. He was once a persecutor who attacked the people of God. He was a violent man who even pursued Christians to their death.

When Paul says he was a blasphemer, a persecutor, and a violent man, he is not exaggerating. Sometimes you hear Christian testimonies and it can sound as if the person is boasting in their sin more than in the cross. That is not what you will find in the testimonies recounted in this book. That is not what Paul is doing here. He is reveling in the power of the gospel to bring change. He was an anti-Christian, anti-church terrorist.

The book of Acts unfolds the story for us. We first meet Paul when his name was Saul, and we meet him on the heels of the glorious sermon that Stephen preached. With the Word of God, Stephen put his finger squarely in the chest of his Jewish audience. The sermon cost Stephen his earthly life for all its brilliant faithfulness to the gospel. Here is the story:

> When they heard this, they were furious and
> gnashed their teeth at him. But Stephen, full of the
> Holy Spirit, looked up to heaven and saw the glory
> of God, and Jesus standing at the right hand of God.
> "Look," he said, "I see heaven open and the Son of
> Man standing at the right hand of God."
>
> At this they covered their ears and, yelling at the
> top of their voices, they all rushed at him, dragged
> him out of the city and began to stone him. Mean
> while, the witnesses laid their clothes at the feet of a
> young man named Saul.
>
> While they were stoning him, Stephen prayed,
> "Lord Jesus, receive my spirit." Then he fell on his
> knees and cried out, "Lord, do not hold this sin
> against them." When he had said this, he fell asleep.

And Saul was there, giving approval to his death.
(Acts 7:54—8:1)

Saul first shows up in the Bible's story line at a mob-style murder, and there he stands giving his approval to the murder. Visions of rapture burst on Stephen's sight; but visions of murder burst in Paul's heart.

This was not a foolish youthful indiscretion done once and forgotten, like a frat boy prank on a college campus. This became Saul's career. He began to give his life to stamping out people like Stephen. Consider Acts 8:1–3.

> On that day a great persecution broke out against
> the church at Jerusalem, and all except the apostles
> were scattered throughout Judea and Samaria. Godly
> men buried Stephen and mourned deeply for him.
> But Saul began to destroy the church. Going from
> house to house, he dragged off men and women and
> put them in prison.

Saul was systematic ("from house to house") and indiscriminate ("men and women"). He was zealous. It's not like the Jerusalem authorities placed a "Help Wanted" sign in the window of the local synagogue. There was no opening for regional persecutor. Paul actually went to the head office and made the case for the creation of the position. Then he made the case that he should be the person that filled the position. "Meanwhile, Saul was still breathing out murderous threats against the Lord's disciples. *He went to the high priest* and *asked him for letters to the synagogues* in Damascus, so that if he found any there who belonged to the Way, whether men or women, he might take them as prisoners to Jerusalem" (Acts 9:1–2, emphasis added). Paul showed initiative in this persecution. He searched under every rock for any who might be a follower of the Way, a follower of Jesus, that he might arrest and imprison them.

Years later, when Paul himself was arrested in Asia, he recalled his former life in words similar to those in 1 Timothy 1: "I persecuted the followers of this Way to their death, arresting both men and women and throwing them into prison" (Acts 22:4). And when appearing before King Agrippa in Acts 26:9–11, Saul again recounted "the before" of his testimony:

> I too *was convinced* that I ought to do *all that was*
> *possible to oppose the name of Jesus of Nazareth* [blas-
> phemer]. And that is just what I did in Jerusalem.
> On the authority of the chief priests I put many
> of the saints in prison, and when they were put to
> death [violent man], I cast my vote against them.
> Many a time I went from one synagogue to another
> to have them punished, and I tried to force them
> to blaspheme. In my *obsession* against them, I even
> went to foreign cities to persecute them [persecutor].
> (emphasis added)

This is the man who pens 1 Timothy and the bulk of the New Testament writings.

Two Questions

The first question that occurs to me when thinking of Paul's before-and-after picture, and whether we have confidence in the gospel to reach the hardest sinners, is this: Why do you suppose Paul continually remembers his past so vividly?

When we think of hardened hearts and hard living of sinners, we must not forget that some sins are not easily forgotten. *Years* have passed and Paul still hears the cries and sees the faces of those he tormented. Sin had left its crimson stain. Sin may be like ketchup spilled on a fresh white shirt. You may be able to wash away the fresh spill itself, but it will leave a stubborn mark. Though sin's stain fades, it lingers and we remember it. As Christians, we may be able to wipe at the stain and remove it to some extent. But those not yet in Christ see and feel that stain of sin. They have a conscience and are aware of it. They may suppress the truth in unrighteousness, but every once in a while the stain of sin raises its head to say, "Here I am." Sometimes the deeper the sin, the deeper the remembrance.

I recall once trying to share the gospel with a lady attending a basketball outreach we have at the church. As I shared, she sort of chuckled incredulously and said, "Honey, God surely gave up on me a long time ago." At that moment, with that thought, even though she didn't know it, she desperately needed *me* to be confident in the gospel's power to transform and to not shrink back in my own unbelief. She had no confidence. So what hope would there be for her if I didn't have hope for her either? She saw the stains of her sin. I needed to sing to her, "What can wash away your sins? Nothing but the blood of Jesus. What can make you whole again? Nothing but the blood of Jesus. Oh precious is that flow that makes you white as snow!"

The second question that comes to mind as I think about Paul is: Why do you suppose Paul threw himself so fully into such a demonic and destructive career as blasphemer, persecutor, and violent man?

In a word, Paul was "lost." It was once quite common for evangelicals to speak of people being "lost." But I don't think I hear that word spoken much anymore. And without that word, we're losing vitally important gospel truth.

What is it to be "lost?" We might define lostness as "convinced blindness and misdirected love resulting in eternal damnation." We see this *convinced blindness* in Acts 26:9–10 where Paul says, "I too was *convinced* that I *ought* to do all that was possible to oppose the name of Jesus of Nazareth. And that is just what I did in Jerusalem" (emphasis added). Paul was convinced. Opposing Jesus was an "ought" for him; he thought it was the right thing to do. Paul thought he could see, but he could not. That is why he tells us in 1 Timothy 1:13 that he "acted in ignorance and unbelief." He does not mean his ignorance was the basis upon which God decided to save him. He is not commending ignorance and unbelief as the path to God's mercy. He is admitting that he was lost. He saw darkness and thought it was light. As Jesus says, "If then the light within you is darkness, how great is that darkness!" (Matt. 6:23). Paul fulfilled Jesus' prophesy that "a time is coming when anyone who kills you will think he is offering a service to God" (John 16:2). That is precisely the kind of convinced blindness afflicting Paul and contributing to his lostness.

But lostness also includes a misdirected love, a misapplied affection. The Lord Jesus summarized the condition of lost man when he said, "This is the verdict: Light has come into the world, but men loved darkness instead of light" (John 3:19). It is not merely that Paul was wrong-headed; he was wrong-hearted also. He delighted in darkness. He delighted in the pleasures of sin even while being convinced of his own righteousness. He was lost and loved it.

Does it matter if we understand and diagnose Paul as lost? Consider how many vitally important gospel truths vanish if we lose any serious grip on the concept of lostness or lose the word that carries the concept. We lose the necessity of repentance because no one is seen as going in the wrong direction. We lose the necessity of substitution because man merely needs to reform himself if man is not lost. We lose the love-worthy majesty of God the Father, God the Son, and God the Holy Spirit because other loves are seen as more satisfying—especially in this right-now, gotta-have-it, materialistic, and worldly life. We lose wrath and hell because if man is not lost then man is not at enmity with God, provoking God's righteous anger and indignation. He is simply on a journey as a seeker, and it would be cruel of God to be angry with or to eternally judge people doing their best to make their way. We lose missions and evangelism because no one really needs to be saved from anything if they are not willfully blind with misdirected affections.

If we lose the concept of lostness, then we lose the whole shootin' match. We lose the entirety of the gospel as critical aspects of the message slowly unravel before our eyes.

But there is a real wrath and a real hell and a real lostness that puts real people in real danger with the only real God. This means we better get real about this truth. We had better preach this gospel in all its unpopular, man-shaking terror and wrath and in all of its sweet, sublime glory. Men and women appear in our congregations every Sunday morning lost in darkest night, thinking they know the way. We must confront them with that gospel that opens their eyes and shows them Christ.

2. The Great Cause of Paul's Change (1 Tim. 1:14–16)

Before, he was a blasphemer, a persecutor, and a violent man. *After,* he is a Christ-appointed, Christ-empowered, thanks-giving apostle of Jesus Christ. How did the change happen? What was the causal agent that transformed Saul into Paul? What was the great cause of Paul's change?

In a word, all this was caused by the gospel of our Lord. The terrorist became an apostle because of the Good News. The apostle Paul writes three things about the gospel that should stir our confidence in the gospel as the means for radically transforming the persons we think are farthest away from Christ.

Paul Tells Us the Gospel Supplied His Need

First, Paul tells us the gospel supplied his greatest needs. Notice how Paul speaks of the gospel as "mercy" in Christ in verse 13. "I was shown mercy because I acted in ignorance and unbelief." Mercy means God punished Paul *less* than Paul's sins deserved.

But Paul also speaks of the gospel as a waterfall of grace, faith, and love. "The grace of our Lord was poured out on me abundantly, along with the faith and love that are in Christ Jesus" (v. 14). I imagine Paul standing at the base of Niagara Falls with its three thousand tons of water rushing over the falls every second—only instead of water it is grace, faith, and love washing over the apostle in the gospel. God's undeserved kindness meant not only that Paul was punished *less* than his sins deserved but also that Paul positively received far *better* than his sins deserved.

All of this mercy, grace, faith, and love were lavished upon Paul "in Christ Jesus." You know, I suspect the apostle Paul wrote so often of being "*in* Christ" because he remained so mindful of the horror of life lived *against* Christ. He had come to know that all the benefits of Christ and all of the blessings of God are bound up in union with Christ. We receive God's blessings and benefits as we are united to his Son by faith. Perhaps Paul meditated on the riches of God's gifts in Christ so often because he remained familiar with the bankruptcy of being without God and without hope in the world apart from Christ. But because he was now "in Christ," united to the Lord Jesus by faith, all Paul once lacked apart from Christ and all Paul regretted of his former life was now completely supplied and reversed in Christ. Notice:

- The blasphemer is given faith;
- The persecutor is now shown mercy and grace; and
- The violent man is made to love.

All of that comes to Paul "in Christ." All that ruined him was renewed "in Christ." For all the sickness and corruption of sin, in the arms of our dear Savior Paul found ten thousand healing charms.

Paul Tells Us the Gospel Is Trustworthy

Second, Paul clearly tells us in verse 15 that the gospel is trustworthy. I love it when God puts the cookie on the bottom shelf where I can reach it by making things plain. We have been meditating on Paul's radical conversion from persecutor to apostle as the basis for our confidence in the power of the gospel. But it is possible that Paul's example is too subtle and I could have missed the need to put my confidence in the gospel for its power to transform the hardest terrorist. But verse 15 makes things very plain: "Here is a trustworthy saying that deserves full acceptance." Let me paraphrase that if I might: *"Hey, knucklehead, place your confidence here on the gospel!"* Verse 15 blinks like a neon sign, beckoning us to enter the certainty of the Good News.

So Paul tells us we should trust the gospel because it supplied all his needs. He tells us we should trust the gospel because it is "trustworthy." The gospel can bear all the weight of our confidence. The message of Christ will not sag under the load of our hopes. The gospel is a steel pillar not only for the church but for our ministry, not only for our conversion but for our preaching. God beckons us to put our trust in the Good News.

What exactly is the message that deserves our complete trust and confidence? Paul tells us: "Christ Jesus came into the world to save sinners." This great announcement is the great cause of Paul's great change. The gospel produced the complete and miraculous conversion of the early church's most notorious terrorist.

Have you ever noticed how often the Bible shrink-wraps the gospel in one tight verse? "For God so loved the world that he gave his one and only Son, that whoever believes in him shall not perish but have eternal life" (John 3:16). "God demonstrates his own love for us in this: While we were still sinners, Christ died for us" (Rom. 5:8). "For even the Son of Man did not come to be served, but to serve, and to give his life as a ransom for many" (Mark 10:45). And here in 1 Timothy 1:15, God packs the message like dynamite into one sentence that explodes into the world and changes people radically.

I once read somewhere that all the information contained in a strand of human DNA could be packaged into the size of a single ice cube, but if the data were translated and written in books it would fill a library. That's what we have in verse 15—a gospel message stuffed and crammed into one sentence that can be stretched in extraordinary length through all eternity to the praise of the riches of his Son! It's all here in one sentence:

- "Christ"—a chosen Messiah, the anointed one from God.
- "Jesus"—the living historical and eternal Son of God.
- "Came into the world"—from where? Glory. From eternity past. How? In the Incarnation.
- To do what? "To Save"—to rescue. From what? The wrath of God coming against man in his sin.
- To save who? "Sinners"—all of Adam's posterity. You and me.

That sentence is pregnant with eternal and glorious truth. Paul says, "Trust it. Preacher, put your confidence in the message."

Paul Tells Us the Gospel Reaches the Worst and that He Is an Example

Third, Paul tells us the gospel reaches the worst of sinners and makes them trophies of God's grace, examples of his saving power. "Christ Jesus came into the world to save sinners—*of whom I am the worst.*"

But lest we think God saving Paul is a unique redemptive event, Paul tells us that he is simply the example meant to inspire others to believe. "For that very reason I was shown mercy so that in me, the worst of sinners, Christ Jesus might display his unlimited patience as an example for those who would believe on him and receive eternal life" (v. 16).

What is Paul saying? Simply this: *God showed me mercy so others would have a faith-inspiring example to look upon and believe unto eternal life.* Paul's life and conversion was simply an object lesson for the rest of us who are stained in our sin and who think, *God gave up on me a long time ago.* If Paul's example is compelling enough to inspire others to believe, then it ought to be compelling enough to inspire our confidence in preaching the gospel itself.

Our "once" of personal sin and lostness serves now to amplify the mercy and grace of our Lord in saving us. The purpose of our unredeemed past is to magnify the greatness of our redeemed present and future in Christ—so much so that others say, "If God saved that guy, I know He will save me."

Do we preach the gospel with that kind of confidence? Do we hold it out to the worst of sinners? Do we think the gospel's reach is shortened by our arm length? No. Put your trust in the Good News.

Consider how our hearts leap with joy and amazement when we hear testimonies of God's grace in someone's life. Each one is the same glorious story of God reaching into time and space to grab sinners to change their hearts and lift them heavenward. Yet how often do we underestimate the gospel to transform even the terrorist; to transform those who once spat in our faces when we shared with them; to transform those whose front yards were littered with beer cans and who lived drunken, drugged lives; to transform those who grew up in the care of faithful Christian parents who simply opened and explained the Scripture in nightly family devotions while living in countries 99 percent non-Christian and hostile to the gospel. These testimonies should move us to deeply rely upon the power of God in the gospel of his Son.

What Would Confidence in the Gospel Look Like?

What should such confidence look like as we minister for our Lord? I have nine concluding applications. You might call these the nine marks of a gospel-confident ministry. If we are confident in the gospel's power to transform:

1. *We will spend time around the worst of sinners looking for gospel opportunities.* Confidence in the gospel brings us into proximity with our "terrorists"—whether in a cross-cultural missions context in a gospel-hostile land or in our settings with our difficult family members and neighbors. We will strategically place ourselves in locations and times conducive to gospel conversation.

2. *We will share the gospel slowly and clearly.* If the gospel does the work, then we only need to release it, unchain it, let it roam and roar through the land bringing light where darkness reigns. Do we think the gospel needs something added to it in order to make it effective? Or do we believe Romans 1:16 that, encased in gospel words, God has packed his power to save even unto the uttermost? Are we trying to release the gospel or are we trying to rehabilitate it?

3. *We will redirect our fears from man to God.* We would fear being *unfaithful* more than we fear being *unfruitful.* Fruitfulness lies in God's hands; faithfulness lies in ours with his help. It is required of stewards that we be found faithful (1 Cor. 4:1–2).

4. *We will endeavor to preach the gospel in every sermon.* On what Sunday do we expect there will be no lost people in our congregations? On what Sunday do we think *Christians* can go without hearing the gospel? If the Good News is our confidence, then we will demonstrate it by appropriately working from every text of Scripture to Christ and to the gospel. The content of our preaching should say every Sunday, "My confidence is in the Good News." The content of our preaching should shout, "I believe you need the Good News of Jesus Christ explained, unpacked, and applied with all the power

that God the Holy Spirit will give us." Our lack of confidence will likely show itself in a desire to say a lot of things *other than* the gospel.

I was reminded of this in my own life when I first preached the sermon that became this chapter. As I heard the sermons and testimonies that came before my own, I kept thinking, "Wow. There goes my sermon right there." Each speaker took some point or nugget that I thought would be my unique contribution. Eventually I leaned over to my wife and said, "I got nothing left." My wife, the godly woman that she is, looked at me and replied, "There's nothing new under the sun anyway, babe."

But I am slow in understanding sometimes. So I returned to the hotel after the first day of conference sermons to work on mine, desiring not to repeat what others said but to say something unique. I sat at my computer praying, "Lord, give me something." And the Lord replied, "Umm . . . excuse me? What's the theme of your sermon?" (The Lord often asks me questions.) I said, "I want to encourage the people to put their confidence in the gospel." The Lord then dropped the bomb: "Why don't you do that too, son."

If we are confident in the gospel's power to transform, we will endeavor to preach the gospel in every sermon. You do realize that God only has one sermon. From Genesis to Revelation, the Lord preaches one message: the redemption of sinners through the atoning work of Christ Jesus his only Son. May we never grow tired of this message.

5. *We will be careful with new converts and with our evangelistic methods.* One way to be careful with new converts is to resist the temptation to view Paul's sudden and dramatic conversion on the Damascus Road as paradigmatic for all subjective experiences of conversion. Don't forget that many people in the New Testament experience conversion as a gradual dawning of truth on the mind and heart. Not everyone is struck down blind on the Damascus Road.

If we don't allow for diversity in subjective experience of conversion we can mishandle conversions and fall to the temptation to adopt unhelpful evangelistic methods. One writer helpfully shows us how restricting subjective experience of conversion can make us hasty with a person's conversion.

> In its evangelistic work the church has sought to replicate in others what happened to St. Paul: a sudden, point-in-time transformation based on an encounter with Jesus. Thus evangelism has focused on a single issue: accepting Jesus as Lord and Savior *now, at this moment in time.* It was assumed that all people at every moment in time were able to answer the question: "Will you accept Jesus?" There was little room for those still on the way in understanding who Jesus is. Evangelistic methods were geared around producing *instantaneous "decisions for Christ."* Mass rallies ended with a call to come forward and make a decision for Jesus. Visitation evangelism dialogues were designed to confront people with the need to accept Jesus *at this moment in time,* lest they die and not go to heaven. Tracts were written that always ended with a prayer of commitment. Certainly the impulse behind such efforts was and is positive. Concerned Christian men and women long for others to enter into the kind of life-changing experience of Jesus they themselves have had. But these evangelistic methodologies are derived from an understanding that the model for conversion is what happened to St. Paul.[1]

What is my point? It is not to disparage a particular evangelistic method or bring it under review. Rather, I am asking: "Is our confidence in our method and visible 'results' or in the gospel which may work beneath our line of sight?" Are we choosing evangelistic methods, perhaps organizing our services in ways that betray the reality that we don't think the gospel is "working" in people's subjective experience? Do we need to see something happen in order to bolster our confidence that the gospel worked?

6. *We will study the gospel in deeper and more varied ways.* If our confidence is in the gospel, we will make ourselves lifelong students of the message, delving deeper and deeper into its riches and its truths. The Good News cannot be exhausted. Here's a suggestion. We might take one aspect of the gospel per month—justice, wrath, substitution, joy, forgiveness, and so on—and research the Bible on how the gospel informs, accomplishes, and lifts up that truth or reality. Search the Scriptures for the entirety of that month peering into the gospel indicatives and imperatives regarding that theme. Roll that aspect of the gospel over in your heart and mind until you see it everywhere you go in the Scripture.

7. *We will preach to open eyes, not just to transfer information.* I gather this point from Acts 26:17–18 where Paul, while recounting his conversion, discusses the commission he received from the Lord Jesus Christ. The Lord spoke to Paul, saying, "I am sending you to them to open their eyes and turn them from darkness to light, and from the power of Satan to God, so that they may receive forgiveness of sins and a place among those who are sanctified by faith in me." The opening of eyes is critical to conversion. Unless there is insight there will not be any turning. Unless people are brought to see that they are lost and headed in the wrong direction, unless they are brought to see that their ideas about God and Christ are wrong, there will be no incentive to turn. So let us pray and labor to understand and communicate the gospel with such fluidity and contact with their lives that we are able, by God's grace and the power of his Word, to bring insight that leads to turning which leads to forgiveness of sin and eternal life.

8. We will ask ourselves, "Is my confidence in myself (preparation, delivery, eloquence, wisdom, etc.) or in the power of the gospel itself?" No doubt, many pastors wrestle with doubt and discouragement at some point after their sermons. I can tell you precisely when it happens to me. About 12:15 p.m. or 12:30 p.m. every Sunday—when I have finished preaching and taken my spot at the church doors to greet people. They walk by saying, "Thank you for the sermon," or "That was a great word." I reply politely, "Thank you; I'm glad the Word of God encouraged you this morning."

But all the while I'm thinking, "I don't believe you; that was terrible. That dog won't hunt. Nothing happened." On Sundays at the church doors I am made freshly aware every week that my heart wants to trust itself, trust my own ability or eloquence rather than trust God and the power of God in the gospel. How subtle is that danger!

Younger pastors especially should learn to recognize this danger of relying on your gifts and preparation rather than the power of God in the gospel. Examine yourself for the telltale signs of overconfidence in self. For me, a lack of confidence in the gospel shows up in frustration, impatience, depression, in a desire to quit prematurely, and in the "fainting spells" when looking for fruitfulness. Beware of the heart's propensity to shift from relying on the gospel of our Lord Jesus Christ to relying on ourselves and what we bring.

9. We will preach the gospel in such a way that our people's confidence would rest not upon the cleverness, cunning, craftiness, and wisdom of men but on the power of God (1 Cor. 2:5). We want to preach the gospel in the Spirit's power, asking the Holy Spirit to give us liberty, freedom, strength, clarity, and specific words and phrases so that our people's hopes and lives would rest upon the omnipotence of God in the gospel and not upon the frailty of men.

3. The Great Celebration that Results from the Gospel (1 Tim. 1:17)

When we live reliant upon and confident in the message of Jesus' death, burial, and resurrection and our union with him through faith, our reliance on the gospel will issue forth in a great celebration. Notice in verse 17 how the apostle empties his testimony in benediction, in doxology, in praise to God. "Now to the King eternal, immortal, invisible, the only God, be honor and glory for ever and ever. Amen."

Paul did not write that sentence with the detached analytical deportment of a systematician. He didn't write that sentence as though compiling a brief systematic theology or list of the attributes of God. He wrote that sentence as someone freshly on the heels of remembering what God has made him to be in Christ.

Verse 17 is a celebration. It is doxology. Seeing the Good News unleashed in the lives and hearts of our congregations should produce celebration and praise to God for all of his eternally glorious attributes and wonderful love. May we see great changes in our people through this great causal agent—the gospel.

Testimony: Hezekiah Harshit Singh

My name is Hezekiah Harshit Singh. I was born and brought up in a gospel-believing family. I read Scripture and prayed every morning and was led in family devotion by my father every evening. Studying Romans at age eleven, I read, "The mind governed by the flesh is death, but the mind governed by the Spirit is life and peace" (8:6 NIV 2011). I went to my mother who explained the meaning of this verse to me, and it was then I prayed to ask forgiveness for my sins and asked Jesus into my life so that I might know this life and peace.

Perhaps this is pretty straightforward testimony for someone born in America perhaps, but for someone born in the state of Uttar Pradesh in north India, such a testimony of growing up in a Christian home is sadly exceptional.

India has a population of 1.2 billion people. There are estimated twenty-five hundred people groups, and over twenty-two hundred of them are still unreached.

Christians make up 2.3 percent of India's population, using the term "Christian" very loosely. But most of them live in the South, leaving the North abandoned of a witness. For example, only 0.18 percent of the two hundred million people living in my state Uttar Pradesh call themselves Christian (again, using the term "Christian" loosely). North India is a factory for false religion: Hinduism, Buddhism, Jainism, Sikh. Fifteen percent follow Islam.

The bondage of idolatry, religious customs, and ageless traditions is massive. Add to this the rampant corruption and widespread extreme poverty of the country. And throw in the "health and wealth gospel" with all of its false promises of riches and healing, and the whole combination is enough to leave anyone standing in the tradition of Adoniram Judson or William Carey feeling hopeless.

But as long as the gospel is true there is hope. My home church, in faith, sponsored and sent me to America to study under faithful pastors and to earn the masters of divinity degree from Southern Seminary.

I am now back in north India, linking arms with a band of brothers to train pastors and plant faithful churches. The gospel that came to me at a young age and changed my life has now called me to this labor of love and sacrifice. And this same gospel is also changing thousands of lives and birthing hundreds of churches in my part of the world, a part which is spiritually dry, dark, and otherwise held in the clutches of the evil one.

Do not underestimate the power of the gospel, either in your own life or in north India.

3

DIVINE SOVEREIGNTY: THE FUEL OF DEATH-DEFYING MISSIONS

David Platt

Scripture quotations in this chapter are from ESV.

I have one overarching truth that I want to communicate as clearly and as biblically as possible, and it is this: *A high view of God's sovereignty fuels death-defying devotion to global missions.*

If we apply this same truth more specifically to pastors, then we might put it this way: *Pastors who believe that God is sovereign over all things will lead Christians to die for the sake of all peoples.*

I believe these two massively important truths spring out of what the apostle John saw in Revelation 5:1–14.

But before we give attention to some implications of John's glorious vision, I want to be clear about three underlying premises that stand behind these truths. Hopefully, by putting these premises on the table at the beginning, I can clarify where I am going, and maybe even disarm you a bit in terms of objections that may already be rising in your mind and heart.

Three Underlying Premises

1. Local ministry and mission are totally necessary (in the life of the church).

I would never advocate the idea that we should neglect local ministry in view of emphasizing global missions. There are people in our churches who are hurting. Their marriages are struggling, their kids are rebelling, and they are walking through cancer and all sorts of other trials. As pastors, we cannot neglect local ministry to our local church body.

Not only is local ministry within the church necessary, but we must also be about local mission in the community. We have been commanded to make disciples, and that command will play out most clearly and consistently in the communities and cities in which we live. In Birmingham, Alabama, the city in which I pastor, there are thousands of people without Christ, and they need to hear and believe the gospel. I want my church to be zealous for the glory of God in Birmingham. Every week I want to encourage every member in our body to make disciples where they live and work and play. This is why we want our small groups to be involved in local ministry. Some of our people are even selling their homes in comfortable suburbia and moving into low-income, high-crime areas in our city for the sake of the gospel. We are sending out church-planting teams to the Northwest, Midwest, and Northeast United States. I only mention these things to say "yes," local mission is totally necessary.

2. Global missions is tragically neglected.

Let me give you some perspective. I was near Yemen not too long ago, where the northern part of this country has about eight million people. That's twice the population of the entire state of Kentucky. Do you know how many believers exist among those eight million people? About twenty or thirty. There are more believers in many Sunday school classes in our churches than in all of northern Yemen. *That* is a problem.

Over two billion people in the world today are classified as "unreached," meaning the gospel is not accessible to them. People say, "Well, there are unreached people all around us," by which they mean "unsaved" people. But that is not what *unreached* means. Unreached does not mean lost. Unreached means that a group has no access to the gospel—no church, no Christian, no Bible available to them. Practically speaking, if you live among an unreached people group, you will be born, you will live, and you will die without ever hearing the gospel that Christians celebrate. And there are two billion people in six thousand different people groups for whom that is a reality at this moment. That is why I say that global missions is tragically neglected.

3. Pastors have the privilege and responsibility to lead the way in global missions.

To quote George F. Pentecost from one hundred years ago: "To the pastor belongs the privilege and responsibility of the missionary problem."[1] Pentecost maintained that mission boards could (and should) do what they do—organize methods, devise movements, and raise money—but it is the responsibility, and privilege, of pastors to feel the weight of the nations and to fan a flame for God's global glory in every local church. I think he was right. The fact that over two billion people in six thousand people groups are not yet reached with the gospel is a problem not primarily for mission boards and mission agencies to address; this is a problem for every pastor and every local church to address.

So let's tie these three underlying premises together. Pastors, we ought to love people in our local churches (local ministry) and in our local communities (local mission) to the end that one day all peoples in all of the world would receive the gospel of God and revere the glory of God (global missions). Ultimately, what drives all of this in the heart of a pastor and in the heart of a local church is a rock-solid confidence in the sovereignty of God. I want to show you how Revelation 5:1–14 speaks to this.

Four Theological Truths from Revelation 5:1–14

Very simply, I want to begin with four theological truths that spring from this passage. Then, based on these truths, I want to conclude by offering four practical implications for pastors. Here is the apostle John's vision:

> Then I saw in the right hand of him who was seated on the throne a scroll written within and on the back, sealed with seven seals. And I saw a mighty angel proclaiming with a loud voice, "Who is worthy to open the scroll and break its seals?" And no one in heaven or on earth or under the earth was able to open the scroll or to look into it, and I began to weep loudly because no one was found worthy to open the scroll or to look into it. And one of the elders said to me, "Weep no more; behold, the Lion of the tribe of Judah, the Root of David, has conquered, so that he can open the scroll and its seven seals."
>
> And between the throne and the four living creatures and among the elders I saw a Lamb standing, as though it had been slain, with seven horns

and with seven eyes, which are the seven spirits of
God sent out into all the earth. And he went and
took the scroll from the right hand of him who was
seated on the throne. And when he had taken the
scroll, the four living creatures and the twenty-four
elders fell down before the Lamb, each holding a
harp, and golden bowls full of incense, which are
the prayers of the saints. And they sang a new song,
saying,

"Worthy are you to take the scroll and to open
its seals, for you were slain, and by your blood you
ransomed people for God from every tribe and
language and people and nation, and you have made
them a kingdom and priests to our God, and they
shall reign on the earth."

Then I looked, and I heard around the throne
and the living creatures and the elders the voice of
many angels, numbering myriads of myriads and
thousands of thousands, saying with a loud voice,

"Worthy is the Lamb who was slain, to receive
power and wealth and wisdom and might and honor
and glory and blessing!"

And I heard every creature in heaven and on
earth and under the earth and in the sea, and all that
is in them, saying,

"To him who sits on the throne and to the Lamb
be blessing and honor and glory and might forever
and ever!"

And the four living creatures said, "Amen!" and
the elders fell down and worshiped. (Rev. 5:1–14)

1. Our sovereign God holds the destiny of the world in the palm of his hand.

This is what John is telling us in Revelation 5:1 when he refers to the "scroll" in God's right hand. This scroll, as we find out in the chapters that follow, contains God's foreordained plans for the future. More specifically, it contains the course of history leading up to the end of the world and the consummation of God's kingdom. This includes God's sovereign will for all creation and ultimate redemption, as well as God's sovereign decrees for the future glorification of believers and the final damnation of unbelievers. And it is all in the hand of God. The last verse of Revelation 4 makes this clear:

> Worthy are you, our Lord and God, to receive glory
> and honor and power, for you created all things, and
> by your will they existed and were created. (v. 11)

Notice that last phrase, "by your will." God is sovereign over nature. The wind blows at his bidding, the light of the sun shines according to his command, and the stars in the sky appear because he calls them each by name. There is not a speck of dust on the planet that exists apart from the sovereignty of our God.

God is also sovereign over nations. He charts the course of countries. He holds the rulers of the earth in the palm of his hand, and this is good news. It is good news to know that Ahmadinejad in Iran is not sovereign over all, and neither is Hamid Karzai or Hu Jintao or Kim Jong-un or Benjamin Netanyahu or Barack Obama. Our God is sovereign over them all.

Finally, we see that God is sovereign over you and me. He creates *all* things, sustains *all* things, knows *all* things, ordains *all* things, and owns *all* things. The Author of creation has authority over creation. He has *all* the rights. That means you and I, as twenty-first-century Americans, don't have rights. God alone has rights.

The unfolding of this scroll reveals that God has the sovereign right to save sinners and to damn sinners. People may ask, "What about man's responsibility? Doesn't man have anything to do with his destiny?" Well, sure he does. Man is certainly responsible in human history, but God is sovereign over human history. An illustration may help to clarify.

Not long ago, I was traveling to Indonesia with J. D. Greear to preach and encourage the saints there. We took different flights, and J. D.'s flight arrived on time, while mine did not. I was delayed for an hour, then two hours, then three hours, and eventually for twenty-four hours. Delta finally got me on a different plane where I experienced *another* delay. At the end of the day, it took me seventy hours to get to Indonesia. As a result, J. D. got to preach some of the sermons that I was supposed to preach, while I was sitting on Delta planes in Delta terminals for seventy hours.

So was God sovereign in this situation? Absolutely. He knew what was going on in Indonesia. He knew that J. D. was a better preacher than I, and that J. D. needed to be preaching those sermons instead of me. God was working in all kinds of ways, doing an infinite number of things. God was sovereign over that whole picture. However, Delta was responsible.

God is in control of creation. God is in control of salvation. God is in control of mission. Therefore, we must remember his sovereign control as we think about global missions. If we aren't careful, we can look at the vast lostness around the world and think to ourselves, "Man, God really needs my help." One of the most shameful moments of my spiritual life involved such a thought. I was hiking in East Asia, going in and out of unreached villages with gospel literature and trying not to get caught. It was a tough, grueling trip. After we had set up camp one night, while a little daylight was left, I went off by myself to read for a few minutes. I had a copy of A. W. Tozer's *The Knowledge of the Holy,* and as I sat down to read it, I looked across the countryside and thought about a hard day of hiking in and out of villages trying to spread the gospel. The thought that came to my mind was this: *God must be glad to have me on his team.* Then, I opened up Tozer's book, where I just so happened to be on the chapter dealing with the self-sufficiency of God. This is what I read:

> Almighty God, just because he is almighty, needs no support. The picture of a nervous, ingratiating God fawning over men to win their favor is not a pleasant one; yet if we look at the popular conception of God that is precisely what we see. Twentieth-century Christianity has put God on charity. So lofty is our opinion of ourselves that we find it quite easy, not to say enjoyable, to believe that we are necessary to God. . . . Probably the hardest thought of all for our natural egotism to entertain is that God does not need our help. We commonly represent Him as a busy, eager, somewhat frustrated Father hurrying about seeking help to carry out His benevolent plan to bring peace and salvation to the world. . . . Too many missionary appeals are based upon this fancied frustration of Almighty God. An effective speaker can easily excite pity in his hearers, not only for the heathen but for the God who has tried so hard and so long to save them and has failed for want of support. I fear that thousands of younger persons enter Christian service from no higher motive than to help deliver God from the embarrassing situation His love has gotten Him into and His limited abilities seem unable to get Him out of. Add to this a certain degree of commendable idealism and a fair amount of compassion for the underprivileged and you have the true drive behind much Christian activity today.[2]

Brother or sister in Christ, let us never forget that God does not need us. He does not need you, and he does not need me. He does not need your church or my church. He does not need "Together for the Gospel." The reality is that all of us, including our churches and denominations and associations, could drop dead and turn to dust, and God would still make a great name for himself among the nations. God involves us in his mission not because he needs us, but because he loves us. In his love for us, he has invited us to be involved in his sovereign design for bringing salvation to the world.

2. The state of man before God apart from Christ is utterly hopeless.

This second truth comes from Revelation 5:2–3:

> I saw a strong angel proclaiming with a loud voice,
> "Who is worthy to open the scroll and break its
> seals?" And no one in heaven or on earth or under
> the earth was able to open the scroll or to look into
> it, and I began to weep loudly because no one was
> found worthy to open the scroll or to look into it.

This scroll, as we've already seen, contains the grand purpose of God in redemption—the ultimate eradication of evil, the defeat of death in the world, and the final removal of sin, suffering, pain, and persecution. This includes the end to all world wars and physical diseases and natural disasters. It also includes the coming of the kingdom of God to man and the re-creation of a new heaven and a new earth, where we will enjoy Christ and reign with him forever and ever. It is all written on the scroll.

And who is able to open the scroll? Who is able to bring these things about? The silence of heaven testifies to the sinfulness of man. There is no one found worthy to open the scroll, and that is why we see John weeping. He gets a glimpse of the state of man before God apart from Christ. Apart from Christ, man has no hope. This is the testimony here and throughout Scripture. Apart from Christ, man is alienated from God (Col. 1:21), under the condemnation of God (Rom. 5:12), enslaved to sin (John 8:34) and in the snare of the devil (2 Tim. 2:26). In his sin, man is the object of God's wrath (Eph. 2:3).

Apart from Christ, man is destined to die forever in hell, a place of fiery agony (Mark 9:43–48), conscious torment (Luke 16:22–24), and continual destruction (2 Thess. 1:9). Hell is a place where the smoke of sinners' torment goes up forever and ever, where they have no rest day or night (Rev. 14:11). The very thought of hell and God's eternal wrath is sobering.

Thomas Watson put it this way: "Thus it is in hell; they would die, but they cannot. The wicked shall be always dying but never dead; the smoke of the furnace ascends for ever and ever. Oh! Who can endure thus to be ever upon the rack? This word 'ever' breaks the heart."[3] Likewise, as people listened to Jonathan Edwards preach in the eighteenth century, they were "urged to consider the torment of burning like a livid coal, not for an instant or a day, but for 'millions and millions of ages,' at the end of which they would know that their torment was no nearer to an end than ever before, and that they would 'never, ever be delivered'"[4]

Oh, see why John is weeping loudly in Revelation 5. This is no casual matter. We say things like, "You played a *hell* of a game," or "That was a *hell* of a song." The way we talk about hell shows that we have no idea what we're talking about. There is a real, eternal wrath awaiting sinners before a holy God, and John knows this. He is audibly wailing at the prospect of the future before God apart from Christ.

Because we have read the rest of the chapter, we know what is about to happen next in Revelation 5. But before we move on, just pause for a moment and contemplate the state of the unreached in the world—people who exist before God apart from Christ. They have never even heard of Christ, but they have heard of God. More precisely, they've seen God. Romans 1:18–20 tells us this:

> For the wrath of God is revealed from heaven
> against all ungodliness and unrighteousness of men,
> who by their unrighteousness suppress the truth.
> For what can be known about God is plain to them,
> because God has shown it to them. For his invis-
> ible attributes, namely, his eternal power and divine
> nature, have been clearly perceived, ever since the
> creation of the world, in the things that have been
> made. So they are without excuse.

Every unreached person in the world has some knowledge of God. Whether it is the man in the African jungle, the woman in the Asian village, the tribe in the Amazon rainforest, or the nomad in the remote desert, they have all seen God. Even if they have not heard the gospel, they have seen God and they have rejected him. Paul describes such people in Romans 1:21–23:

> For although they knew God, they did not honor
> him as God or give thanks to him, but they became
> futile in their thinking, and their foolish hearts were
> darkened. Claiming to be wise, they became fools,
> and exchanged the glory of the immortal God for
> images resembling mortal man and birds and ani-
> mals and creeping things.

People ask me, "What about the innocent guy in Africa who has never heard the gospel—what happens to him when he dies?"

I say, "He goes to heaven, without question." The only problem is . . . *he doesn't exist*. There is no innocent guy in Africa. If he existed, he would not need the gospel, for he's *innocent*. He would go to heaven because he has no sin. The problem is that there are no innocent unreached people in the world. Every unreached person in the world stands guilty before God. That is why they need Christ.

There are over two billion people in the world at this moment whose knowledge of God is only sufficient to damn them to hell forever. They have knowledge that he exists, but they have rejected him. They deserve his wrath, and that is the end of the story for them. They have never even heard that there is a Redeemer. These people exist before God apart from Christ, and in that state they are utterly hopeless. But there is hope!

3. The greatest news in all the world is that the slaughtered Lamb of God reigns as the sovereign Lord of all.

After weeping, John hears good news:

> And one of the elders said to me, "Weep no more;
> behold, the Lion of the tribe of Judah, the Root of
> David, has conquered, so that he can open the scroll
> and its seven seals." (Rev. 5:5)

The words of the elder remind us of the One who was promised centuries ago to the patriarchs of old. This Lion from the tribe of Judah will receive "the obedience of the peoples," according to Genesis 49:10. The reference to the "Root of David" points us back to Isaiah's prophecy: "There shall come forth a shoot from the stump of Jesse, and a branch from his roots shall bear fruit. And the Spirit of the LORD shall rest upon him . . . [and he] shall stand as a signal for the peoples" (Isa. 11:1–2, 10). Likewise, Jeremiah makes this prediction: "I will raise up for David a righteous Branch, and he shall reign as king" (Jer. 23:5). The Lion of the tribe of Judah and the Root of David has come, and he has conquered. Weep no more!

Throughout history, men and women have come and gone, the noblest, the kindest, the strongest, and the greatest of them. All of them have fallen prey to sin as slaves of Satan. Generation after generation, century after century, every single man and woman has succumbed to death. But then came another man who was unlike any other. This man did not fall prey to sin; this man possessed power over sin. This man was not enslaved to Satan; this man crushed that ancient snake. This man did not succumb to death; this man triumphed over death. This is why Paul can say,

> "O death, where is your victory? O death, where is
> your sting?" The sting of death is sin, and the power
> of sin is the law. But thanks be to God, who gives us
> the victory through our Lord Jesus Christ. (1 Cor.
> 15:55–57)

So we see that Christ has conquered, but how? How did Jesus conquer sin and death?

John turns around to see the strong Lion, and behold, he sees a slaughtered Lamb. This is the same apostle who recorded John the Baptist's reaction to Jesus: "Behold, the Lamb of God, who takes away the sin of the world!" (John 1:29). This language hearkens back to Exodus 12, when the Israelites took an innocent lamb into their homes, kept it until the fourteenth day, and then killed it and spread its blood over their doorposts. The people of God were saved from the judgment of God under the banner of the blood of a lamb.

Centuries later, Isaiah speaks of a lamb who would be led to the slaughter (Isa. 53:7). The prophet tells us that the Son of God would be crushed according to the will of the Lord (Isa. 53:10). So, how would this Lion conquer? By suffering as a Lamb. By paying the penalty due our sin and by experiencing the condemnation due our souls. He was marred, despised, rejected, stricken, smitten, afflicted, wounded, chastised, oppressed, and pulverized in our place. All who

hide under the banner of his blood will be saved. Jesus is the slaughtered Lamb of God, and yet . . . he is standing.

The Lamb of God has not only endured death in our place, he has
also defeated death in our place. The One who is sovereign over death
bears the scars of death. The hymn writer has said it beautifully:

> *Crown Him the Lord of love;*
> *behold His hands and side,*
> *those wounds, yet visible above,*
> *in beauty glorified.*
> *All hail, Redeemer, hail!*
> *For Thou hast died for me,*
> *thy praise and glory shall not fail*
> *throughout eternity.*
>
> *Crown Him the Lord of life,*
> *Who triumphed o'er the grave,*
> *and rose victorious in the strife*
> *for those He came to save.*
> *His glories now we sing,*
> *Who died, and rose on high,*
> *Who died eternal life to bring,*
> *and lives that death may die.*[5]

Jesus has risen from the grave with all power and authority in
heaven and on earth. His seven horns depict his might and his seven
eyes depict his ability to see all things, know all things, and uniquely
accomplish all things. In Revelation 5:7, we are astonished to read
that Jesus "took the scroll from the right hand of him who was seated
on the throne." Breathtaking audacity, isn't it? No one in heaven or
on earth or under the earth is able to take the scroll, and yet Jesus
walks right up to the throne, surrounded by living creatures and
elders and a host of angels, and he takes it. The slaughtered Lamb of
God reigns as the sovereign Lord of all.

You may say, "I thought God was sovereign, but now you are saying that Jesus is sovereign." Yes! Is there any clearer picture of the divinity of Christ than his authority to accomplish the sovereign will of God while angels praise His name? God doesn't share the spotlight with just anyone. In fact, he only shares the spotlight with himself, so it's significant how he relates to Jesus. When Jesus humbled himself as a Lamb, he became:

> . . . obedient to the point of death, even death on
> a cross. Therefore God has highly exalted him and
> bestowed on him the name that is above every name,
> so that at the name of Jesus every knee should bow,
> in heaven and on earth and under the earth, and
> every tongue confess that Jesus Christ is Lord, to the
> glory of God the Father. (Phil. 2:8–11)

This is the greatest news *and* the greatest paradox in all the world. Salvation through sacrifice. The consummation of God's kingdom comes about through the crucifixion of God's Son. Apparent defeat gives way to astonishing victory. And there is hope for all peoples! All of this leads to the fourth theological truth springing from this text.

4. The atonement of Christ is graciously, globally, and gloriously particular.

Notice the "new song" that the four living creatures and the twenty-four elders sing in Revelation 5:9–10:

> Worthy are you to take the scroll and to open its
> seals, for you were slain, and by your blood you
> ransomed people for God from every tribe and lan-
> guage and people and nation, and you have made
> them a kingdom and priests to our God, and they
> shall reign on the earth.

Oh, what a *graciously* particular atonement. In the words of Ephesians 1:3–11:

> Blessed be the God and Father of our Lord Jesus
> Christ, who has blessed us in Christ with every
> spiritual blessing in the heavenly places, even as he
> chose us in him before the foundation of the world,
> that we should be holy and blameless before him. In
> love he predestined us for adoption as sons through
> Jesus Christ, according to the purpose of his will, to
> the praise of his glorious grace, with which he has
> blessed us in the Beloved. In him we have redemp-
> tion through his blood, the forgiveness of our tres-
> passes, according to the riches of his grace, which he
> lavished upon us, in all wisdom and insight making
> known to us the mystery of his will, according to
> his purpose, which he set forth in Christ as a plan
> for the fullness of time, to unite all things in him,
> things in heaven and things on earth. In him we
> have obtained an inheritance, having been predes-
> tined according to the purpose of him who works all
> things according to the counsel of his will.

Christian, feel the weight and wonder of this. God purposed to save you. Christ purposed to purchase you. Amidst your weakness, amidst your struggles, amidst your suffering, amidst trying moments in your family, amidst conflicts in the church, and amidst days that you want to quit, don't forget this: Before the sun was ever formed, before a star was ever placed in the sky, before mountains were ever laid upon the earth, before oceans were ever poured upon the land, Almighty God set his sights on your soul. And he sent his Son, according to the purpose of his sovereign will, to purchase you for him. That's a graciously particular atonement.

When we consider this graciously particular atonement in the context of the unreached people groups in the world, it is even more amazing. There are people—billions of them—who are born, who live, and who die without ever hearing the gospel. Yet you and I have been born into a time and place where we have heard the gospel. We had nothing to do with this. God, in his sovereign mercy, ordained that your life and my life would be counted among the reached and, if you are a Christian, the saved. So, yes, it is a graciously particular atonement.

But it's also a *globally* particular atonement. Christ has not just purchased you and me; he has purchased people for God from every tribe and every language and every people and every nation. All of them. And remember, the Bible is not just talking about nations like we think of them, as in the approximately two hundred geopolitical nations recognized in the world today. That is not what is being talked about here. The reference is to tribes and families and clans and peoples—what we refer to today as people groups.

We see this idea of people groups all over Scripture: Amorites, Hittites, Perizzites, Canaanites, Hivites, and Jebusites. Today, this would include the Baluch, the Berber, the Hui, the Han, and the list goes on and on. Over eleven thousand of these people groups are spread throughout the world. These are groups of people that share a similar language, a similar heritage, and certain cultural characteristics. And Jesus died to purchase men and women from every single one of them. His atonement is globally particular.

This globally particular atonement is why Jesus told us to make disciples of "all nations" in Matthew 28:19. This is not just a general command to make disciples among as many people as possible; rather, it is a specific command to make disciples among every people group in the world. Make disciples of all the people groups.

So brother or sister in Christ, if there are over six thousand people groups that have still not been reached with the gospel of

Christ, then we have missed the point of the atonement. Our obedience to the Great Commission of Christ is incomplete, because our commission is not just to make disciples. Our commission is to make disciples *of all the nations.*

The sovereign will of God is that people from every single people group will be ransomed by Christ. Therefore, the sovereign command of Christ for you and I is to make disciples among every people group on the planet. That is the point of the atonement. Particular atonement drives global missions. If we believe Revelation 5:9, that Jesus died to purchase people from every tribe and tongue and nation, then we will go to every tribe and tongue and nation. We will go and make disciples of all the people groups.

People may ask, "Aren't we just guilting people into going to unreached peoples?" That is a good question. Why do we go and make disciples of all the people groups? Is it because we feel guilty that we are reached? Because we feel guilty for all the resources we have? No.

What drives our passion for unreached peoples is not guilt; it's glory. It's glory for our King. We believe that our sovereign God deserves the praise not just from *some* of the people groups on the planet, but from *all* the people groups on the planet. And we are not going to stop until every single people group purchased by Christ is giving him the glory he is due. That is what drives us.

The atonement of Christ is not only graciously and globally particular, but it is *gloriously* particular. In his sovereignty, God is gathering together a kingdom of priests who have been purchased for his praise from all languages, all colors, and all clans. Can you see it? The beauty of every single ethnic group in the world gathered around one throne, joined by "myriads of myriads and thousands of thousands, saying with a loud voice, 'Worthy is the Lamb who was slain, to receive power and wealth and wisdom and might and honor and glory and blessing!'" (Rev. 5:11–12). Every ethnic group in the world joining "every creature in heaven and on earth and under the earth and in the sea, and all that is in them, saying, 'To him who sits on the throne and to the Lamb be blessing and honor and glory and might forever and ever!'" (Rev. 5:13). Amen. That is what we live for. That is what we die for. *A high view of God's sovereignty fuels death-defying devotion to global missions.*

Four Practical Implications for Pastors

Based on the truths that we have seen in Revelation 5, I want to challenge pastors who know that our God holds the destiny of the world in the palm of his hand, who feel the weight of man's utter hopelessness before God apart from Christ, who have had their eyes and hearts opened to the greatest news in the all the world—that the slaughtered Lamb of God reigns as the sovereign Lord of all, and who believe that the atonement of Christ is graciously, globally, and gloriously particular. Pastors, if these things are true, then what shall we do? Does a belief in divine sovereignty mean we sit back and do nothing? Are we to passively float in the sea of God's sovereignty while he accomplishes his purpose in the world? No! Instead, I want to suggest four practical implications for pastors in response to our text.

1. Let us lead our churches to pray confidently (for the spread of the gospel to all peoples).

God's sovereignty does not negate prayer; God's sovereignty necessitates prayer. We skipped over this point in Revelation 5:8, and it is similar to what we see in the following chapters of Revelation. When the seventh seal is opened, this is what we see in Revelation 8:3–4:

> And another angel came and stood at the altar with
> a golden censer, and he was given much incense to
> offer with the prayers of all the saints on the golden
> altar before the throne, and the smoke of the incense,
> with the prayers of the saints, rose before God from
> the hand of the angel.

Pastor, did you catch that? God has sovereignly ordained the prayers of his people to bring about the coming of the kingdom. That is, God will consummate his kingdom ultimately and eternally in gracious response to our prayers.

So let us teach and lead our people to pray, "Your kingdom come." Tell them what Matthew 24:14 says—that "this gospel of the kingdom will be proclaimed throughout the whole world as a testimony to all nations, and then the end will come." Tell them this truth, and then lead them to pray for the end to come. Lead them to cry for the end to come, for the gospel to go to the nations. Show them how to use *Operation World* to pray for every nation and people group in the world: Saudi Arabs and Iranian Turks and the Lohar of South Asia and the Somalis of North Africa and the Brahman of India. And assure them, as they pray, that every one of their prayers is piling up at the altar of God until one day, at the appointed time, he will bring his kingdom and accomplish his will on earth as it is in heaven.

Assure your people that one day, when all the nations have been reached with the gospel, the end is going to come. People ask, "Do you really believe that?" My response is, "Well, Jesus said it." Or they ask, "How do you know when a people group is officially reached? Are you saying that Jesus couldn't come back today, since there are six thousand people groups that are still unreached?"

No. That is not what I am saying. Jesus could definitely come back today. We do not know for sure exactly what is meant by the terms "people groups" or "reached." These are simply our best estimates when it comes to the *ethne* of the world. Yet I cannot improve at this point on the words of George Ladd, who referred to Matthew 24:14 as "the single most important verse in the Word of God for the people of God today." He explains it this way:

> God alone knows the definition of terms. I cannot precisely define who all the nations are, but I do not need to know. I know only one thing: Christ has not yet returned; therefore, the task is not yet done. When it is done, Christ will come. Our responsibility is not to insist on defining terms; our responsibility is to complete the task. So long as Christ does not return, our work is undone. Let us get busy and complete our mission.[6]

Let's lead our people to pray for God's kingdom to come. Let's lead them to plead for the day when all peoples praise his name.

2. Let us lead our churches to give sacrificially.

According to one estimate, Christians in North America give an average of 2.5 percent of their income to the local church. In turn, churches in North America give an average of 2 percent of those funds to overseas missions efforts. This means that for every $100 a North American Christian makes, he or she gives $0.05 through the local church to the rest of the world. Five cents!

I recently wrote a foreword for a revised edition of *When Helping Hurts* by Steve Corbett and Brian Fikkert. Near the beginning of that book we read these words: "The Bible's teachings should cut to the heart of North American Christians. By any measure, we are the richest people ever to walk on planet earth."[7] I read that, and I've got to ask the question, "Why?" Why are we the richest people ever to walk on planet earth? Why has God given us, and our churches, so much? I'm convinced Psalm 67 is the answer:

> May God be gracious to us and bless us and make
> his face to shine upon us, that your way may be
> known on earth, your saving power among all
> nations. . . . The earth has yielded its increase; God,
> our God, shall bless us. God shall bless us; let all the
> ends of the earth fear him! (vv. 1–2, 6–7)

The blessing in Psalm 67 is, at least in part, material. And the reason for this material blessing is clear: God gives his people worldly wealth for the spread of worldwide worship.

Pastor, does your church budget reflect a priority on the spread of the gospel? How about the spread of the gospel to unreached peoples? Remember Matthew 6:21: "For where your treasure is, there your heart will be also." If you put your money in more stuff and more programs and more things for those in the church, then your heart will follow. On the other hand, if you put your money in missions, then your heart will likewise follow. So let us lead our churches to give sacrificially. The sovereign God of the universe has willed for us to be wealthy for the sake of his worship.

3. Let us lead our churches to go intentionally (to all peoples).

Pastor, are the people in your church going to unreached peoples? Are *you* going to unreached peoples? Let's lead our churches to send a variety of different people through a variety of different avenues to a variety of different people groups around the world. Let's lead them to send people short-term, mid-term, and long-term. Each of these methods can be effective.

There are certainly foolish ways to do short-term missions—trips that pass for little more than Christian tourism, or trips that actually hinder gospel work in some places. But there are also wise ways to do short-term missions, partnering together with long-term disciple-makers and long-term disciple-making processes around the world. For example, I can think of a short-term team we recently sent to the largest unevangelized island in the world. There were fifty different people groups there, but no church on the island. So, we sent a team to work with a gospel partner on that island, and the gospel partner sent this team hiking with a couple of translators into remote villages among one of these unreached people groups. The team went hiking and praying, asking God to do what he did in Lydia's life, to sovereignly open somebody's heart to believe (Acts 16:14–15). And the sovereign God of the universe did just that.

This team had the opportunity to share the gospel with a household in this remote area of the most unevangelized island on the earth, and upon hearing of Christ, the family in that household believed on him. That is the power of the articulated gospel. Our partners and translators have followed up since then, and a church has now formed among this people group. It is the first church and the first group of Christians in this *ethne*, this people group, and we praise God that we got to be a part of it. Once people start getting in on God's global plan like that, they will want more.

Mid-term is the classification we use to refer to people who go out for a time period ranging from two months to two years. We are sending out as many high school and college students as we can on mid-term missions. We call it the "mormonization" of the Church at Brook Hills, except we are going with the true gospel. And it is not only high school and college students who are going, but also retired and semi-retired brothers and sisters, including teachers who are off during the summers. We are trying to send out anyone who is able to go.

At the end of the day, we want all of our missions efforts to be fueling long-term missions. This involves people packing their bags, selling their possessions, and moving overseas to plant their lives among unreached peoples.

There is no question that in the New Testament we see both Timothy-type ministers and Paul-type missionaries. Timothy-type ministers are those whom God calls to stay in a church (among the reached) and shepherd the body, while Paul-type missionaries are those whom God calls to leave the reached and scatter to the unreached.

Pastor, there are men and women in your church whom God is calling to Paul-type ministry. Maybe not everybody, but some of them. God is calling them to pack their bags and move overseas to spread the gospel among unreached peoples. So are you encouraging them? Are you calling them out? Are you coming alongside them? Are you taking time during the year in your preaching and in your pastoring to speak specifically to them? Are you leading the church to fast and pray like those in Antioch in Acts 13:1–3? Have you prayed, "God, who are you calling out next to go long-term to unreached people groups overseas?" And then are you waiting and listening until he answers? Are you listening and asking God if *you're* one of the ones he might be sending out?

When I talk about sending people out, I'm not just talking about traditional missionary routes that we might think of. Yes, those are certainly crucial, but I'm also talking about vocation as mission, like a businessman and a school teacher in our church who said, "Hey, we can teach school and do business among people who have no access to the gospel, so let's go to the people who have no access." I'm talking about people using their gifts, their skills, and their passions for the sake of global missions. People can use their training in medicine and business and sports and education to fan out among the nations for the sake of God's fame.

People say, "Well, aren't there local Christians who can do this work better than us? Why don't we just send them money and let the locals do it?" But that misses the point. In these places, there are no locals—no local Christians and no local churches. That is what it means to be unreached. And God's design is not for you and me to send them our money so they can lose their lives spreading the gospel instead of us. All of this leads to the final, and most important, implication.

4. Let us lead our churches to die willingly.

We lead our churches to pray confidently, give sacrificially, go intentionally, and ultimately to die willingly. Again, a high view of God's sovereignty fuels death-defying devotion to global missions. Pastors who believe that God is sovereign over all things will lead Christians to die for the sake of all peoples.

Oh, pastors, unreached peoples today are unreached for a reason. They are difficult to reach. They are dangerous to reach. Many of them don't want to be reached, and they will oppose anyone who tries to reach them. How, then, does Revelation 5:1–14, and the picture of God's sovereignty contained in this passage, fuel death-defying missions to dangerous people groups?

We have already seen how God's sovereignty compels us to go to unreached people groups. Jesus has purchased them for himself, so we are compelled to go. However, we are not only compelled to go because of God's sovereignty, but we are also *confident* as we go. We know that when we go to dangerous people groups, nothing can happen to us outside of the sovereign will of a good and gracious God. Nothing. When the church first experienced persecution in Acts 4, they prayed, and the first words out of their mouth were, "Sovereign Lord" (v. 24). They knew that their persecutors could do nothing to them except that which God in his sovereignty would allow. This is crucial.

One Romanian pastor who was interrogated, abused, and beaten for proclaiming Christ said that what got him through it all was a high view of God's sovereignty. It was the realization that those soldiers who questioned him and beat him could do absolutely nothing

to him that God did not allow them to do. The pastor, Dr. Josef
Tson, recounted one occasion when he was being interrogated by six
men, and he said this to his interrogators:

> "What is taking place here is not an encounter
> between you and me. This is an encounter between
> my God and me."
>
> The interrogators look puzzled, and Tson said,
> "My God is teaching me a lesson [through you]. I
> do not know what it is. Maybe he wants to teach me
> several lessons. I only know, sirs, that you will do to
> me only what God wants you to do—and you will
> not go one inch further—because you are only an
> instrument of my God."
>
> Tson then remarks, "To see those six pompous
> men as my Father's puppets!"[8]

Yes!

When we send out church-planting teams from our church to go
and live among dangerous people groups, we are sending them out
with confidence, because we know and they know that nothing can
happen to them apart from the sovereign hand of God who desires
their good and *his* glory.

"But," you might ask, "won't they suffer? Won't it be difficult?"
Of course it will. And why is that? Because the sovereign design of
God for the spread of the gospel in the world includes suffering. It
always has. We know this from Revelation 5, where we see that God
ordained the suffering of his Son for the salvation of the world. We
also know this from Revelation 6:11, where we see that God has sovereignly ordained a set number of martyrs to be killed for the spread
of the gospel. When we put these truths from Revelation 5 and 6
together, we realize: Jesus suffered to provide the gospel; we suffer
to propagate the gospel.

Obviously, this doesn't mean we seek suffering or martyrdom, but it does mean that as we seek Christ and proclaim Christ to the ends of the earth, there will be suffering and there will be martyrs, and it will all happen in the sovereign design of God. This is clear throughout the book of Acts. How did the gospel go to Judea and Samaria? Through the stoning of Stephen (Acts 8). Stephen looked up and saw the sovereign Son of Man standing at the right hand of God as he was being pelted with rocks (Acts 7:55–58). Then God, in his sovereign will, used Stephen's death to scatter the church to the ends of the earth. Satan's strategy to stop the church only served to spread the church.

Consider also Paul's example. Whenever he was facing danger, it was the sovereignty of God that kept him going. While in Corinth in Acts 18, the Lord said to Paul, "Do not be afraid, but go on speaking and do not be silent" (v. 9). And why shouldn't Paul be afraid? The Lord said, "for I have many in this city who are my people" (v. 10). Or, recall Paul's farewell to the Ephesian elders in Acts 20. Paul says the following:

> And now, behold, I am going to Jerusalem, constrained by the Spirit, not knowing what will happen to me there, except that the Holy Spirit testifies to me in every city that imprisonment and afflictions await me. But I do not account my life of any value nor as precious to myself, if only I may finish my course and the ministry that I received from the Lord Jesus, to testify to the gospel of the grace of God. (vv. 22–24)

Paul embraced suffering as part of God's sovereign design for the spread of the gospel, which forces us to ask, "Will we do the same?" Pastors, will we lead people in our churches to embrace suffering as

part of God's sovereign design for the spread of the gospel? Will we
lead them to die willingly?

Hear again from the Romanian pastor I referenced earlier. He
tells this story:

> During an early interrogation at Ploiesti I had told
> an officer who was threatening to kill me, "Sir, let me
> explain how I see this issue. Your supreme weapon
> is killing. My supreme weapon is dying. Here is
> how it works. You know that my sermons on tape
> have spread all over the country. If you kill me, those
> sermons will be sprinkled with my blood. Everyone
> will know I died for my preaching. And everyone
> who has a tape will pick it up and say, 'I'd better
> listen again to what this man preached, because he
> really meant it; he sealed it with his life.' So, sir, my
> sermons will speak ten times louder than before. I
> will actually rejoice in this supreme victory if you kill
> me."
>
> He sent me home.
>
> Another officer who was interrogating a pastor
> friend of mine told him, "We know that Mr. Tson
> would love to be a martyr, but we are not that foolish
> to fulfill his wish."
>
> I stopped to consider the meaning of that state-
> ment. I remembered how for many years, I had been
> afraid of dying. I had kept a low profile. Because I
> wanted badly to live, I had wasted my life in inactiv-
> ity. But now that I had placed my life on the altar
> and decided I was ready to die for the gospel, they
> were telling me they would not kill me! I could go
> wherever I wanted in the country and preach what-
> ever I wanted, knowing I was safe. As long as I tried

to save my life, I was losing it. Now that I was willing to lose it, I found it.[9]

I was with a group of believers in a difficult part of the world
recently and we spent part of one day commemorating a brother and
two sisters who had been shot and killed in a hospital where they
were working. These three servants moved there for the spread of the
gospel among this people group, knowing they would face opposition. However, nothing could have prepared them for the day when
a man walked into that hospital with a fake bandage on his hand
and a blanket wrapped around his arm made to look like a baby.
He entered the office area and immediately unwrapped the blanket
to reveal a loaded rifle. Starting in the office and working his way
through the rest of the clinic, he killed all three of these believers.
When authorities asked this guy why he did it, he said, "If those
people kept doing what they were doing, people all over this country
would believe in Jesus." What was most interesting, though, is that
shortly before this incident, the mission organization that these missionaries were with had considered pulling them out of that country
for safety concerns. And the woman who was eventually shot had
said to her supervisor, "Whatever you do, don't pull me out of the
country. You will kill me if you pull me out."

She and the other two missionaries knew that suffering and death
were possibilities, but they believed it was worth it. They died willingly. But why? What causes that kind of death-defying obedience to
reaching the peoples of the world? Confidence in the sovereignty of
God. Confidence that nothing can happen to you apart from his sovereign will. Confidence that he is wise, and that in his wisdom God
may ordain our earthly death for others' eternal life. God did this, by
the way. In the aftermath of that shooting, sixty-three believers were
found gathered together in secret house churches in that country as
a result of the ministry of that one woman.

In the midst of suffering, we have confidence that God is going to use even persecution for the eventual accomplishment of the Great Commission. Every single, every couple, every family, and every team we send to work among dangerous unreached people groups knows with confidence that when this gospel is proclaimed, people are going to be saved. That's a guarantee. Every people group is going to be there in Revelation 5 and 7—every nation, tribe, and tongue in the world. Therefore, we can go to the hardest people group on the planet, preach the gospel, and know that at some point, whether in our life or through our death, somebody's coming out. And the reason we know this is because Christ has already purchased them for God. Do you see how God's sovereignty provides unshakable, death-defying confidence in the face of dangerous people groups?

Pastors, let us be finished and done with puny theology that results in paltry approaches to global missions in the church. Let us believe deeply in the sovereign God of the universe who holds the destiny of the world in the palm of his hand. Let us see the hopeless state of man before God apart from Christ, and let us lead our churches to pray, to give, and to go to unreached peoples with the greatest news in all the world. We have been saved by a graciously, globally, gloriously particular sacrifice, so let us lead our churches and let us give our lives—let's lose them, if necessary—for the advancement of Christ's kingdom and the accomplishment of Christ's commission. And let's not stop until the slaughtered Lamb of God and sovereign Lord of all receives the full reward of his sufferings.

Testimony: Matthias Lohmann

My name is Matthias Lohmann. I didn't need God. That, at least, is what I thought growing up. I was not against Christianity. Having grown up in the Lutheran State Church in Germany, I even considered myself to be a Christian. But I had never heard the gospel.

When I was twenty-five years old, I met a girl. I liked her and asked her out. But she turned me down. She told me that, as a believer, she wouldn't date a non-Christian and that she certainly had quite different ideas of dating than I did. I couldn't believe it. I was convinced she had overly protective parents. Eventually she agreed to meet me—at her parents' house—in order to tell me why she questioned my claim to be a Christian. I arrived being absolutely convinced that I would be able to talk her out of this.

She told me the gospel.

I left confused, realizing that she really knew what she was talking about and that I had no clue about these matters. It became clear to me that I was not a Christian and I began to wonder whether I should be.

Months went by and I continued to live my happy worldly life. But God was drawing me. Nearly a year later, I went to a church service with this young lady. A few days later, in January 1998, I woke up one morning shaken and changed. God had revealed himself to me. I knew he existed. And I knew I had to turn to him for the forgiveness of my sins and a new life. By God's sovereign grace I was converted.

A few years later I started taking seminary classes while I remained in my business career. In 2008, I finally left my business job and became the pastor of a church in downtown Münich. Every day, I see people all around me who think they don't need God. Today it is my life's ambition to preach the gospel to these people.

In the life of people who think that they don't need God, don't underestimate the power of the gospel!

4

SPIRIT-POWERED, GOSPEL-DRIVEN, FAITH-FUELED EFFORT

Kevin DeYoung

Unless otherwise noted, Scripture quotations in this chapter are from ESV.

The Young, Restless and Reformed movement is known for many things. We are, I hope, known for our commitment to the gospel, for our belief in the inerrancy of Scripture and expositional preaching, for our celebration of the doctrines of grace, for our convictions about biblical manhood and womanhood, and for our unwavering defense of penal substitution and justification by faith alone.

But for all that is good about the New Calvinism, there are at least two critical areas of doctrine and life where we have yet to show the necessary interest and enthusiasm. One is an earnest commitment to global mission, a stirring among ourselves and a bold call to others to go to the least reached peoples of the world and share the gospel. The other area of relative neglect is a passion for personal holiness.

A Necessary Holiness

According to Hebrews 12:14 holiness is not optional for the Christian. Rather, we must "strive for peace with everyone, and for the holiness without which no one will see the Lord." This holiness cannot be referring to our positional righteousness before God because the verb is "to strive." Hebrews exhorts us to strive for a progressive personal actual holiness without which we will not see the Lord. There are not many things as important as this statement. Do you want to be one of those who see the Lord in this life and in the next? Then you must be holy. If we do not have at least a desire, a yearning, a fight for holiness, then we ought to wonder if we are saved.

Is your life, is your church, is this wonderful Reformed resurgence marked by a striving after holiness? Puritanism has been called a reformed holiness movement. Would anyone think to call us the same? As we rightly celebrate all that Christ has saved us *from*, let us also think often about, and strive earnestly for, all that he has saved us *to*. Those most passionate about the gospel of God's free grace should be those most passionate about the pursuit of godliness.

This chapter is not so much about the *ought* of holiness. I hope you are convinced of that already. These pages are about the *how* of holiness. There are many Christians who sit in our churches every Sunday who have a desire to grow in godliness. They want to be transformed from one itty-bitty degree of glory to the next. They desire to make some progress on the way to the celestial city. What can be said to help them on that journey? How will you help them get there? How will you stir them up to love and good deeds? Will you give them legalism? Will you give them license? Will you give them platitudes? How do we make progress in piety, and how can we assist others in the same?

A Grace that Works

First Corinthians 15 is famous because in it Paul gives a succinct and powerful summary of the gospel. And as he explains the gospel—giving historical fact plus theological interpretation—his summary culminates in the resurrection of Christ. In verse 5 he begins listing those who saw the risen Lord: Cephas, the twelve, five hundred brothers at one time. Finally he says in verse 8 that the Lord Jesus Christ appeared "also to me." Paul is thinking of his Damascus Road experience. He, too, saw the resurrected Christ, though in a different way. Paul acknowledges he is last and least of the apostles: last because he saw Christ after the others, and least because he once persecuted the church.

But then notice what Paul says in verse 10: "By the grace of God I am what I am." He may be last and least, but everything he is now and has been doing is a gift from God. And yet, this grace is not opposed to personal exertion. Paul says two things at the end of verse 10 which seem contradictory, but are not. In fact, if we are to flourish as ministers of the gospel and indeed as Christians at all, we must hold these two things together. Paul says on the one hand, "I am working very hard. What I have done, what I am doing, is the result of hard work. I have busted my rear to teach and read and plant churches and study the word and be a man worthy of my calling." But then says, "Hold on just a second. I want to be clear that everything I just said about me trying, working, making an effort—that is God's grace in me. I am working because God is at work."

We must understand this point. Our work is not only a *response* to the grace of God; it is the *effect* of the grace of God. The key to Christian ministry and the Christian life is understanding that (1) we need to work hard, and (2) God's grace is at work in us.

Or to put it another way: growth in godliness requires spirit-powered, gospel-driven, faith-fueled effort.

That is a nice phrase, isn't it? Sounds almost Piperian with all those hyphens. But what does it actually mean? In real life, how is the pursuit of holiness powered by the Spirit, driven by the gospel, and fueled by faith?

Being Careful with Clichés

I'm a big sports fan. I like to play them in a feeble manner and I like to watch them when I get a chance. So I have seen a lot of sports' interviews in my day. Sometimes the athlete is very poised and articulate, a model of wisdom and humility. At other times . . . not so much. Anyone who has watched a lot of sporting events understands that the pre- or post-game interview is not always where you go for the deepest thinking and the most insightful commentary.

Sometimes the reporter is to blame for the banality. Have you ever noticed they don't ask questions, they just recap the event and then put a microphone in someone's face? As the athletes are walking off the field at the end of the game a reporter will saddle up to the star wide receiver and say something like, "You caught a pass at the fifty-yard line, slipped past the safety, outran the corner, and then angled to the pylon as time expired—give me your thoughts." What do you expect the poor guy to say? His thoughts were, *There are a lot of people chasing me right now and I should run real fast.* You can't expect him to say, "Well I was really thinking about Dostoevsky's greatest works and Orwell's *1984* and their connection to *The Hunger Games.*" Not likely.

What is likely is that you will hear the same old phrases over and over. When the coach is asked for his strategy, the reply is usually along the lines of, "We want to win the turnover battle." Oooh! Brilliant! Let me write that down. Or maybe: "We just want to keep our head in the game and take it one game at a time." Are these really revolutionary strategies? As if there has ever been any coach anywhere in the history of sports whose strategy was to keep his team's heads in the clouds and take it three games at a time. Perhaps these clichés communicated something useful at one time, but now they are so overused and worn out that they don't say much of anything.

As Christians we can speak in the same types of generalities. It is not that I want to censor certain words or phrases, but let's admit that some phrases don't sound impressive and communicate little. "You need to just give it over to God." What does that mean? Are you taking something to the post office? To the bank? Or what about: "You have to bathe it in prayer; soak it in the Spirit; wash it in the Word." Sounds very clean, but what does any of this mean? I'm not saying our clichés are unbiblical or untrue, but they can also be relatively unhelpful. We need to help people understand what our fine-sounding phrases actually mean and how they practically work in real life. So what does it mean to say sanctification comes by spirit-powered, gospel-driven, faith-fueled effort? What does this look like? How does it work?

Spirit-Powered

Let's take each phrase in turn, starting with "Spirit-powered."

First Peter 1:2 speaks of the "sanctification of the spirit." Since the third person of the Trinity is the Holy Spirit, it makes sense that he would play the lead role in making us holy. The Spirit not only sets us apart in a definitive positional sense, he also progressively sanctifies us to become increasingly like Christ. To understand how he does this, consider two biblical images for the Spirit.

The first is the Spirit as power. Ephesians 3:16 makes a remarkable claim: "[God the Father,] according to the riches of his glory[,] may grant you to be strengthened with power through his Spirit in your inner being." There's a supernatural power at work within you!

The same Spirit present at creation is at work in your inner being, giving you a heart that *wants* to resist sin and a will that *can* resist sin. The same Spirit who raised Jesus from the dead dwells in us to give life to our mortal bodies (Rom. 8:11).

You may think to yourself: *I have problems. I have sins. I have addictions. I have struggles.* Well, you may, but you also have the Spirit that raised Jesus from the dead working within you. He is not a little weak spirit. He is not like a cute Casper the friendly ghost. Some Christians think the Holy Spirit is nothing more than an exuberant guy sort of floating around helping people lift up their hands. Make no mistake: there is nothing weak or little or sleight about the Spirit. He is a strong Spirit, a Spirit of power, not a little vapor, but a mighty rushing wind. Defeatist Christians who do not fight against sin because they figure "I will never change" or "I don't have enough faith" are not being humble. They dishonor the Holy Spirit, who strengthens us with supernatural power. The Spirit gives us the strength to do what we could not do on our own.

The second image is of the Spirit as light. In John 16:8 Jesus says he will send the Spirit to convict the world concerning sin, righteousness, and judgment. Elsewhere in John the word "convict" is translated "exposed" (John 3:20). Jesus is saying the Spirit will expose the world's rebellion. That is part of Spirit-powered sanctification. He turns on the lights so we can see what we have been blind to.

Have you ever been in a room in your house, or in the attic or garage, and you flip on the light switch and the floor moves? Not a good feeling. No one likes to be surprised by little rodents or insects or snakes scurrying beneath you. Why does that happen? Why do they run away so vigorously? Because someone turned on the lights. They want to be in the dark. They want to be hidden. They have no desire to be out in the open. Sin is like that too. People love darkness rather than light because their deeds are evil (John 3:19). This is what happens when you really preach with conviction and when God works in your life with conviction. Rats of sin are going to scurry. Cockroaches are going to run up the walls and look for a dark place to hide. Sin does not want to be in the light. But it is the mercy of God to shine a spotlight nonetheless. That is part of what you are trying to do when you teach and preach. You are shining a giant spotlight on sin.

Here is a prayer that God has always answered in my life—sometimes a week later, sometimes a day later, sometimes five minutes later—"Lord, show me my sin." He will always answer that prayer. I've prayed it before saying, "God, I don't know if I mean it, but I want to mean it, so I'm praying it again. Please show me my sin." Ask him to turn the lights on. The Spirit exposes sin.

The Spirit also reveals truth. Every Sunday we have something in our bulletin called a "prayer of illumination." It comes right before the sermon. It is a prayer for light. Before I preach I always pray that God would enlighten our eyes and lead us into the truth (John 16:13). This is the work of the Spirit.

Every pastor has had the experience of someone coming up after the message and saying, "That sermon was just for me. You were speaking right to my heart." And every pastor has had the experience of thinking to himself, "I didn't know I was saying that." It's not that the people are making things up. They are simply hearing a better sermon than the one that was preached. That is the Spirit shining a light on the truth of their sin and the truth of the Word. How else can it be that you preach the same sermon and two people with very different needs, in very different circumstances, both conclude that God was speaking right to them in the sermon? How does that happen? Not because the preacher is so smart or the pastor is wire-tapping the phone or trolling around on Facebook. It is the Spirit at work to apply and reveal the truth.

And finally, as light the Spirit exposes the glory of Christ. He does not just throw a spotlight on sin and illumine the truth; he also draws our attention to Jesus. This is one reason why any notion of anonymous Christians won't work. Unfortunately, even the great C. S. Lewis espoused this idea in both *Mere Christianity* and *The Last Battle*. He thought that people might be drawn unknowingly to Christ and be Christians without calling on Christ or knowing anything explicitly about him. Likewise, some people will argue that if you really believe in the sovereignty of God, then you must acknowledge that the Spirit can blow wherever he wills and save people in surprising ways. Well, that's certainly true. The Spirit is mighty to save, but when he regenerates the heart and converts the sinner, it is never apart from throwing a spotlight on the glory of Christ. Whenever he saves, he also shines. That is why 2 Corinthians 3:18 is so precious: "And we all, with unveiled face, beholding the glory of the Lord, are being transformed into the same image from one degree of glory to another." We become what we behold. You look at Christ to become like him.

The Spirit sanctifies us by revealing our sins, revealing the truth, and revealing Christ. If the Spirit has been flipping the light switch in your heart, don't crawl back under the covers. That's what the Bible calls resisting the Spirit, quenching the Spirit, or grieving the Spirit. If you are doing this, you are looking for the darkness because you cannot stand the light. You don't want to think about your sin or think about Christ. May the Spirit overcome our blindness and impotence. He is our power and our light. Spirit-powered sanctification means God is gracious to show us our sin, show us our Savior, and strengthen us to live a different way.

Gospel-Driven

Everyone agrees that the pursuit of holiness must flow from the gospel. But how does the flow work? How do good deeds grow out of Good News? This is where we need to connect the dots for our people and help them see what goes on in the heart when the gospel drives us toward holiness.

Let me give you two examples.

First, the gospel drives us to godliness out of a sense of gratitude. This is the point of Romans 12:1: In view of God's mercies present ourselves as living sacrifice. This is not some kind of debtor's ethic where we repay God for what he's done for us. Paul makes it explicit that the Christian life is lived in response to grace—that's gratitude. Those of you with kids or grandkids understand what gratitude looks like. It may be short-lived, but when a child gets a present there is immediately a sense of gratitude at that moment when the gift has been given. Even in the hardest little heart there is a newfound desire to please, an eagerness to be warm and kind.

When I travel I like to bring something back for my kids. I got a text the other day from my oldest son. He is only eight but we are bad parents so our children sometimes grab the phone and text. Yesterday he wrote, "Dear Daddy, could you send me pictures of three Louisville slugger bats and I will pick one out. Thanks. Love, Ian." Wow, how do you say no to a text like that? And if I bring home a bat for him, the first thing I will have to do is clear out the other four children so they don't get smacked in the head. But after that I know my son will say, "Thank you, Daddy." He will be genuinely grateful. And from that gratitude he will be eager to please me, eager to maintain a good relationship with me. That is the response of gratitude when you have been given grace. The humility and happiness that comes with gratitude tends to crowd out whatever is coarse or ugly or mean. There's not enough room for nastiness when you have gratitude. If you have an anger problem or a bitterness problem, no matter what else is going on in your heart, you can be sure you also have a gratitude problem.

I am often convicted of this because I think this is true of many parents. I struggle with impatience and irritability with my kids. I was convicted lying awake one night after I had blown up at one of my children: "Lord, how ungrateful. They're kids. They're sinful kids. They're my kids. You've given them to me as gifts." All I could see was the way in which my life had been made more difficult with children. I didn't see how much better my life was too. So what was my sin? There was anger and impatience, but at the root of it was a profound sense of ingratitude. I wasn't holy because I wasn't thankful.

Second, the gospel drives us to godliness by telling us the truth about who we are. Certain sins become more difficult when we understand our position in Christ. If we are heirs of the whole world, why do we envy? If we are God's treasured possession, why are we jealous? If God is our Father, why would we be afraid? If we are dead to sin, why live in it? If we have been raised with Christ, why continue in our old sinful ways? If we are seated with Christ in the heavenly places, why do we live like we belong somewhere else?

It is easy to become convinced that we can never change. People every Sunday think that. "God gave up on me a long time ago. He forgave me seven times, maybe even seven times seventy. But I need more than that. I'm beyond the reach of God's grace." This where you must do spiritual warfare with the sword of the Spirit. Fight back with the truth of the gospel. Remember that there is no con-demnation for those who are in Christ Jesus (Rom. 8:1). Remember that the Spirit of him who raised Jesus from the dead is at work within you (Rom. 8:11). Remember that you are a child of God, and if a child, then an heir (Rom. 8:16–17). Remember that nothing can separate you from the love of God which is in Christ Jesus our Lord (Rom. 8:38–39).

The gospel motivates us by reminding us to be who we are. The pursuit of holiness starts with embracing our identity in Christ. You have probably heard of Lady Gaga and may know that one of her most famous songs is "Born This Way." The message of the song is what you think it would be. It's a celebration of every personality, gender preference, and sexual choice. Don't let anyone judge your actions because you were "born this way." The message defines our culture. And whenever there is something that resonates with people made in the image of God, you have to wonder if there is a half-truth here and a very damnable lie. And so it is with this song. It's true: you must be who you are. You cannot be someone you are not. How can you ask someone to deny their very person? That is what the world thinks and it's close to the truth. Our identity matters. Who we are defines what we do. But the Good News of the gospel is that no matter how we are born, we can be reborn a different way. If we are in Christ, we must (and can!) live like Christ (Col. 2:6). The gospel drives us toward godliness.

Faith-Fueled

We must not think justification is all about faith but that sanctification has nothing to do with faith. It is not as if we are justified by faith and then we put faith behind us and just have to screw up our courage and try to be better. No, we are justified *by* faith and in a different sense sanctified *through* faith. Here is where we must be more careful with our language. Sometimes in an effort to really exalt the grace of God, we will say that we are also sanctified by faith. But you must be very cautious with that kind of language because in order for that to work you must mean something different with the word "by" than you do in justification "by" faith.

The faith in justification is a faith that rests and receives. The faith in sanctification is one that wills and works. So if you say we are justified *by* faith and we are also sanctified *by* faith, you might be saying something misleading. The word "by" in the first instance (related to justification) means we receive a right standing before God and are counted righteous through no effort of our own. That is what we mean by faith alone. But if we say we are sanctified by faith alone, what would that mean? Does it mean we receive a holiness without any striving or effort? We must understand faith plays a role in sanctification, but that doesn't mean the same phrases for justification can be imported to the realm of sanctification. Better to say, as Scripture says, that the pursuit of holiness is the fight of faith (1 Tim. 6:11–12).

The struggle to grow in godliness is fueled by belief in the gospel, belief in our identity in Christ, belief in God's Word, and belief in his promises. Take a look at the Sermon on the Mount for example. Start with the Beatitudes. You will hear promise after promise meant to fuel your fight for holiness. "Blessed are the meek, for they shall inherit the earth" (Matt. 5:5). That's a promise. If God promises that the meek will inherit the earth, then why I am spending my whole life to be somebody, to have something to show for myself? Maybe you are in ministry for that reason. You want to be a success. You want to prove something to the world. You want a reward. Jesus does not say, "Well, just forget about it." He says, "You want to be somebody? You want to have something? I'll tell you how. Be meek. I won't guarantee you'll have a big church, or a big house, or a big family. I promise you something better. I'll give you the whole earth."

Or think about Matthew 5:8—"Blessed are the pure in heart, for they shall see God." This verse more than any other has helped me in my battle against lust and second looks. Back in the day I used to walk to work. One day I saw out of the corner of my eye a young woman washing her car in the driveway. I won't describe the scene in detail, but suffice it to say this young lady was not wearing a "modest is hottest" T-shirt. So when something of this scene caught my eye, there was a temptation. A temptation to look, to turn my head, to sin. The fight at this moment was a fight of faith. And this verse was singularly powerful for me. "Blessed are the pure in heart, for they shall see God." I would walk by and think, *I want to see God. I want to see God today. I want to know God better. I don't want to rob myself of the opportunity to see God, now, today, to know his presence, so I will not look over to my left.* That is faith-fueled sanctification—to believe the promises of God. That helped me keep my head down. I believed God had a better vision for me.

The holy life is always the life of faith. Believing not just in our justification, but believing with all our heart what God has promised to us now and will be ours in the future. And then acting as if all that were really true.

God-Given, God-Glorifying Effort

Before I talk about the role of human effort, keep in mind everything I have already stated. We must rely on the Spirit. We cannot save ourselves. We have to keep fighting with the power of better promises. The call of Christian preaching should never be to make people better, more virtuous or moral, apart from the power of the Spirit, the truth of the gospel, and the centrality of faith.

And at the same time, the realities of the Spirit, the gospel, and faith do not eliminate the need for human effort. As we saw in 1 Corinthians 15:10, Paul worked hard, though it was the grace of God at work within him. Do not let "effort" be a four-letter word in your Christian vocabulary. Romans 8:13 says, "By the Spirit [we must] put to death the deeds of the body." Ephesians 4:22–24 instructs us to put off the old self and put on the new. Colossians 3:5 commands us to put to death what is earthly in us. First Timothy 6:12 urges us to fight the good fight. Luke 13:24 exhorts us to strive to enter the narrow gate. First Corinthians 9:24–27 tells us that we are running a race, we are training, we are beating our bodies. Philippians 3:12–14 talks of pressing on and straining forward. Second Peter 1:5–7 tells us make every effort to add to your faith, knowledge and kindness and brotherly love. And Jesus himself in

Revelation 2 and 3 promises that the reward of eternal life go to those, and only those, who conquer.

Christians work. As J. C. Ryle put it, the child of God has two great marks about him: his inner peace and his inner warfare. We are at rest with God but we are never at rest with sin and the flesh and the devil.[1] *Striving, fighting, wrestling*—these are good Bible words and they have a good lineage in church history. Listen to Calvin:

> As it is an arduous work and of immense labor to off the corruption which is in us, he bids us to strive and make every effort for this purpose. He intimates that at no place is to be given in this place for sloth and that we ought to obey God, not slowly or carelessly but that there is need of alacrity as though he had said, put forth every effort and make your exertions manifest to all.[2]

Charles Hodge says,

> In the work of regeneration, so new birth, the soul is passive, it cannot cooperate in the communication of spiritual life. But in conversion, repentance, faith and growth in grace, all its powers are exercised. As however the effects produced transcend the efficiency of our fallen nature and are due to the agency of the spirit. Sanctification does not cease to be supernatural or a work of grace because the soul is active and cooperating in the process.[3]

So we should not say that sanctification is monergistic. I am not sure synergism communicates the right meaning either, but monergism is certainly not the proper phrase for progressive sanctification. The term protects an important biblical truth when it comes to *regeneration*, but theologians have not used these terms in discussing sanctification. The Bible teaches that in our new birth there is only one working (monergism) and that is God. But in sanctification we have to say that we work as God works through us. Great theologians like Calvin and Hodge were not at all ashamed to say the Christian puts forth effort. We co-operate with God. According to Herman Bavinck, God gives us the gift of sanctification in a passive way,[4] but in a different sense, people are called and equipped to sanctify themselves. God works in us and then we work it out (Phil. 2:12–13).

We must understand that when it comes to sanctification we cannot simply tell people "look to the Lord." We must say more than "get gripped by the gospel." We must also say "Work hard. Put forth effort." We do not want to fall into the error of the old Keswick theology of "let God and let God." Sanctification is not by surrender but by divinely enabled toil and effort.

The Hardworking Pastor

This means, among other things, that pastors should be prepared to work hard. Remember that in 1 Corinthians 15:10 Paul is talking about how hard he works as an *apostle*. There is application in his words for all of life, but his first concern is to relay how much he has labored for the gospel. As pastors we work long hours, we work long weekends, and we work with deep hurts and sins. Of course, the work is also glorious. It is the best job I can imagine. When I think of brothers who work on the line at GM six days a week or sisters who raise a family almost singlehandedly, I have little patience for pastors who feel sorry for themselves. But I want to remind my friends in ministry that they should expect to toil hard and labor long. You will have to leave your vacation to do a funeral. Your day will get obliterated by a crisis. You will be criticized unfairly. You will miss not having the luxury of knocking off early on Friday and taking a long weekend at the cottage. You and I must be prepared to work hard for the gospel, just as Paul did.

One of our most enjoyable and most difficult efforts will be the weekly grind of preaching. Preparing a message (or two or three) every week is a labor of love, and sometimes the emphasis is on the labor. Not every sermon is going to be a homerun. Sometimes you just hope for a bloop single or a chance to bunt your way on. You're going to have those weeks (months?) where you stare at the text and don't know what to do with it. The longer you are in ministry the easier the preparation comes because you have more tools and more experience. But it also gets harder because you realize you have preached on Ephesians fifty times before. You have to keep reading, learning, and growing. Otherwise you will get bored with preaching and people will get bored with your sermons. When people ask how long they should spend on sermon preparation, I like to say, "As long as it takes for your soul to be ignited."

I have often thought there is something truly godlike in doing sermons. Don't take that the wrong way. I don't mean preachers are like gods. But the process of making something out of nothing is one powerful way to image the Divine. That's what preaching is. You stare at a blank sheet of paper or a blank screen and you have to create something ex nihilo. It takes hard, creative work. You have got to be rested. You have got to be walking with the Lord to do this well week after week. You have to struggle.

Just listen to Paul in Colossians 1:28–29: "Him we proclaim, warning everyone and teaching everyone with all wisdom, that we may present everyone mature in Christ. For this I toil, struggling with all his energy that he powerfully works within me." Do you hear what he is saying? Ministry is toil. Struggle to proclaim Christ. We struggle to present others mature in Christ. We do all this with Christ's energy, but that does not mean it is not tiring.

I know there is the danger of becoming workaholics and neglecting our health and family. I sense those temptations in my own life. But the antidote to working too much is not to work less. In fact, if we are workaholics it is probably because we are lazy in some important area of our lives. It is not possible to work too hard, just like it's not possible to say you're focusing on the gospel too much, or you're talking about grace too much. But we can become imbalanced. We can talk about grace in a shallow way or a truncated way. And we can approach hard work with the same imbalances. The problem is not working too hard, but working foolishly. Or perhaps we are only working in one area of life. We gladly toil at the office, but we never work hard to disciple our children or cherish our wives. Pastors who work too much may assume the problem is they need a break. And that is probably part of it. But just as much, we may need to work harder at feeding our souls, caring for our families, and saying no to lesser priorities.

Trust and Obey

If we as pastors do not challenge ourselves to put forth effort, we will be even more timid to challenge our people. I think many of us are getting to a point where we are scared to tell people that the Bible would have them do some things and not do other things. The Bible is full of commands, in both Testaments. If we do not preach the imperatives, we are not preaching the Bible. Think of the Great Commission. Part of our missional marching orders is teaching people to obey. If we are not interested in obedience—ours and others'—we are not taking the Great Commission seriously. In Romans 16:19, Paul praises the church because their obedience is known to all. Would any describe our churches in that way? Would we even want them to? Maybe we would rather be known for our music or our gym.

I understand that talk of obedience raise concerns about the dangers of legalism. No doubt, legalism can be a huge problem. We don't want Christians thinking they are right with God because of what they do, and we do not want churches that always talk about what we need to do and never celebrate what God has already done. But there is another problem out there. It is antinomianism. The word means against law (*anti-nomos*). Hard-core antinomians tell people it doesn't matter how they live. Grace becomes a license for licentiousness. That's one obvious manifestation of the problem. A more subtle strand of antinomianism simply refuses to tell people how to live. They do not deny that holiness is important, but they don't want to talk about effort. They will not dare tell people that how you live now might keep you out of heaven later.

We might call this tendency *nomophobia*, fear of the law. We know the law can convict us of sin and lead us to Christ, but for all practical purposes we have lost the third use of the law, the law as a pattern for righteousness. This is not about earning anything. It is about living out who we are by God's grace. Remember that the law in the Old Testament came after the gospel. God did not say to the Israelites enslaved in Egypt, "I want you to get things right and clean up your act for fifteen years and then I'll save you." No. He said, "I will come. I will deliver and send you out so that you can worship me." And then he gives them the law. So theologically we cannot only say that law leads us to the gospel; we can also say that law comes after gospel.

Exhortation Is Not Anti-Gospel

We should not be afraid to tell people what the Bible says over and over again, that they must obey commands. If you preach on David and Bathsheba and you never say anything about great David's greater son, the Lord Jesus, and you never say anything about God's mercy for adulterers, then you are not connecting the dots. You are not bringing the gospel to bear on people's struggles. You are not giving any Good News. But if you preach on David and

Bathsheba and you don't say anything about sexual sin, then you are not preaching the text. The chapter ends by announcing, "The thing that David had done displeased the LORD" (2 Sam. 11:27). If you are going to preach 2 Samuel 11 faithfully and exegetically, you should talk at length about how sin displeases the Lord and how we should not commit adultery or give ourselves over to little sins that lead to big, life-altering sins.

Or let's say you are preaching on Luke 18. Jesus gives us the application right up front: he told the parable so that they would always pray and not lose heart. How do you preach that? Now there's a legalistic way to preach it and you just kind of lean over and say, "You people do not pray. Do you love God? If you did you would pray more. God knows how meager your prayer life is. Shame on you." That's a life-destroying way to preach. But it would also be a mistake to turn this text into nothing but a message on how God forgives us even when we don't pray. "Look at Jesus. He is the great prayer warrior fighting for us when we fail." That's all gloriously true, but it is not exactly the point of the story. Jesus tells the parable so we will keep praying. So the sermon ought to be about diligence in prayer. And if you look carefully at the text and work hard at your sermon you will see there is a gospel way to preach on this exhortation. You might talk about the word "elect" and how our identity motivates us to pray, or how God is a just judge and faithful Father so we can believe in the power of prayer. There is plenty of Good News to announce from this passage, while at the same time not shortchanging the implicit command.

The Grace that Leads Us Home

Our preaching will be greatly helped if we remember to preach not just the content but the mood of the text. You cannot assume that everyone in your church needs a kick in the pants or that everyone in your church needs a hug. You have to preach the text. Let the sweet texts sing sweetly and let the stern warnings sound stern. You have to pray for the Spirit to work and give each person just what they need. Give them grace every week, without fail, without exception. But make sure it is the grace that saves a wretch like me and the grace that leads us home.

I was working on the conclusion of my sermon one week and realized that I was going to land on these themes of hard work and effort. We were having Communion that Sunday. At first I thought, *I have to change the order of my points. I need to put effort first and then end with something more gospely. I cannot emphasize hard work and then lead people to the table.* But then I realized, if it's not grace-filled or gospel-centered to exhort God's people to obedience, then I should not do it at all, no matter where it falls in the sermon or what kind of service it is.

Making an effort to be holy is not sub-Christian or anti-gospel. The gospel is the Good News of salvation and it has three tenses. It is the message that God saved you from the wrath of God, God saves you unto holiness, and he will save you for glory. It is all of grace. So don't give people half a Savior. Don't give them a half a glass of grace. Give them grace all the way down and all the way home. When you come to the exhortations and commands of Scripture, you are not leaving grace behind. It is grace that forgives you and grace that changes you.

Think of the benediction in Hebrews: "Now may the God of peace, who through the blood of the eternal covenant brought back from the dead our Lord Jesus, that great Shepherd of the sheep, equip you with everything good for doing his will, and may he work in us what is pleasing to him, through Jesus Christ, to whom be glory for ever and ever. Amen" (13:20–21 NIV 2011). What is the God of resurrection power doing in this passage? He promises to equip you with everything good for doing his will. He is at work within us so that we might will and do according to his good pleasure. The God who justifies promises to sanctify.

> *Rock of Ages, cleft for me, let me hide myself in thee. Let the water and the blood from thy wounded side which flowed. Be of sin the double cure. Save for guilt and make me pure.*

These issues matter because some of us are stalled out in our sanctification for lack of effort. We need to know of the Spirit's power. We need to be rooted in gospel grace. We need to believe in the promises of God. And we need to fight, strive, labor, toil, and make an effort to be holy. That is what 1 Corinthians 15:10 is all about. Without faith in the gospel and the power of the Spirit and the grace of God at work within us, we are just teaching pigs to fly. But without the biblical exhortation to effort, we will be confused and discouraged, wondering why sanctification does not just automatically flow out of us because we are so in love with justification. The danger is that we will be waiting around for enough faith to get the gospel, when God wants us to get up and work as he works within us.

Here are the two indispensable truths when it comes to sanctification: holiness does not happen apart from trusting, and trusting does not put an end to trying.

Testimony: John Joseph

My name is John Joseph. The words "total immersion" would describe my relationship with sin from the earliest of ages. The nature and degree of my sin grew more grievous with each passing year. My sin defined me. I became an alcoholic, a drug user, and a drug dealer. I dishonored my parents. I was a liar. I used everyone and everything for personal gain, and was full of lust, greed, and hate.

In late 2008, while at Blockbuster, I came across Bill Maher's mockumentary entitled *Religulous*. After watching the documentary I was annoyed at Maher's obvious bias in his portrayal of religion, and so got onto the web search engine Google in order to search for a debate on Christianity. What I found was Ravi Zacharias, and over the course of the next year, Ravi would completely dismantle everything I believed in.

As I continued to search for more teaching on the web, God, in his mercy, would eventually lead me to Desiring God Ministries. On January 5, 2010, I sat down to listen to a message on John 3:16. Prior to beginning the sermon, Mr. John Piper prayed that someone would be brought from the darkness and into the light. Being faithful and true, our Father answered that prayer. Not five minutes into the message, I sat devastated by the reality of my sin and the impending judgment that awaited. But I was also overwhelmed by the knowledge that my sins could be forgiven through the blood of Jesus Christ—all of them! I repented and believed.

Our heavenly Father's kindness and mercy did not stop at salvation. He has continued giving in ways beyond what I could ever imagine. He eventually led me to Capitol Hill Baptist Church, where, through sound teaching and fellowship, he has caused me to grow and has changed my heart to want to serve him in every area of my life, for the rest of my life, and for the glory of his name.

Had you seen me in 2008, you would have likely said, "He is unreachable." But now by grace I am a testament to the power of the gospel. There is not a soul in this world that is too lost or too dead or too far from God's reach. Tell everyone this gospel. This gospel is not to be underestimated.

5

FALSE CONVERSIONS: THE SUICIDE OF THE CHURCH

Mark Dever

Scripture quotations in this chapter are from NIV 1984.

For those who have heard of me, I am often associated with the topics of church membership and discipline. What I want to offer here is a kind of prequel of how I became this way, and it has to do with why the gospel is underestimated today in too many cities, even in too many churches.

The matter at hand is false conversions, which I believe are the suicide of the church. Consider Paul's words in 1 Timothy 4:16: "Watch your life and doctrine closely. Persevere in them, because if you do, you will save both yourself and your hearers." This text raises a question for those of us who are pastors: Could it be that many of our hearers are not saved? Even many of our church members?

In fact, I believe there is a significant problem of false conversions in our churches. An illustration can be found in the autobiography of mid-twentieth-century poet and novelist Langston Hughes. He recounts a crucial teenage experience:

> I was saved from sin when I was going on thirteen.
> But not really saved. It happened like this: There
> was a big revival at my Auntie Reed's church. Every
> night for weeks there had been much preaching,
> singing, praying, and shouting. . . . Finally all the
> young people had gone to the altar and were saved,
> but one boy and me. He was a rounder's son named
> Westley. Westley and I were surrounded by sisters
> and deacons praying. It was very hot in the church,
> and getting late now. Finally Westley said to me in
> a whisper, 'G* d*! I'm tired o' sitting here. Let's get
> up and be saved.' So he got up and was saved. Then
> I was left all alone on the mourner's bench. My aunt
> came and knelt at my knees and cried, while prayers
> and songs swirled all around me in the little church.
> The whole congregation prayed for me alone, in a
> mighty wail of moans. . . . God had not struck West-
> ley dead for taking his name in vain or for lying in
> the temple. So I decided that maybe to save further
> trouble, I'd better lie, too, and say that Jesus had
> come, and get up and be saved. So I got up. Sud-
> denly the whole room broke into a sea of shouting,
> as they saw me rise. . . . I couldn't bear to tell her
> that I had lied, that I had deceived everybody in the
> church, that I hadn't seen Jesus, and that now I didn't
> believe there was a Jesus any more. . . .[1]

To the best of my knowledge, Langston Hughes remained a committed atheist throughout his life.

Now, some might ask, "What's the problem with false conver-sions as long as other people, at the same time, are really getting converted? After all, aren't the Gospels full of images that suggest that we should not worry about this too much?"

Most famously, Jesus' parable of the sower in Mark 4 gives four examples of the Word being rightly sown, making no distinction in what is sown or how it is sown. But in three of those examples, the result is taken away, falls away, or is choked out. Doesn't this suggest that Jesus understands that some people will appear to respond positively to the Word, but prove over time that they are not spiritually alive and crop-producing? Why would we try to avoid what Jesus promised will happen? False converts are inevitable.

In the early church, the Donatists tried to over-purify their congregations with disastrous results. And in general, a fear of false conversions could lead us to be too cautious. Too careful. Suspicious of grace. Overzealous in inspecting fruit. Even self-righteous and legalistic! Surely it is better to promiscuously preach the gospel to everyone in every way.

One might recall what D. L. Moody famously quipped to the critics of his evangelistic methods: "I like my way of doing evangelism better than your way of not doing evangelism."

In short, if the Bible tells us that there will be both opposition to the truth and false-positives, why should we give time to fixing what is inevitable in gospel ministry?

But the experience of Langston Hughes is just one example of what I fear—merely in our nation—must be many thousands, if not many millions, of people who have been received into our churches unconverted. In fact, I want to argue that there is a problem, indeed, a serious problem. And then I want to consider what might done about it, especially if you are a pastor.

To that end, we will look first at the *plan*, then the *problem*, then the *source of the problem*, and finally a few *practical suggestions*.

God's Plan

We begin by considering God's overarching plan to bring glory to himself through a people. God's plan begins to unfold when he calls the idol-worshipping pagan, Abram, and promises him, "all peoples on earth will be blessed through you" (Gen. 12:3). What's more, we eventually learn that the nations of the earth will be blessed as God reveals his glory through his people. Thus David commands, "Declare his glory among the nations, his marvelous deeds among all peoples" (1 Chron. 16:24; cf. Ps. 18:49).

The Psalms are full of such language. Psalm 22 tells us, "All the ends of the earth will remember and turn to the LORD, and all the families of the nations will bow down before him" (v. 27; cf. 45:17). And Psalm 46:10, which many people know, begins, "Be still, and know that I am God." But do you know how it ends? "I will be exalted among the nations" (Ps. 46:10; cf. 47:7–9). I also love the preview of the book of Revelation found in Psalm 86: "Among the gods there is none like you, O Lord; no deeds can compare with yours. All the nations you have made will come and worship before you, O Lord; they will bring glory to your name. For you are great and do marvelous deeds; you alone are God" (vv. 8–10; cf. Ps. 102:15).

This is God's plan—to make himself known and exalted among the nations!

This is what he promises in Malachi: "'My name will be great among the nations, from the rising to the setting of the sun. In every place incense and pure offerings will be brought to my name, because my name will be great among the nations,' says the LORD Almighty" (1:11, cf. 14). And this is what is gloriously fulfilled in Revelation, where the four living creatures and the twenty-four elders fall down and sing a new song to the Lamb "because you were slain, and with your blood you purchased men for God from every tribe and language and people and nation" (5:9). This great multitude appears two chapters later, described as "a great multitude that no one could count, from every nation, tribe, people and language, standing before the throne and in front of the Lamb" (7:9).

If it is God's plan to bring glory to himself, how will he do it? To answer that, we should start back in Genesis. Before he dies, Jacob prophecies of a ruler who will come in the line of Judah: "The scepter will not depart from Judah, nor the ruler's staff from between his feet, until he comes to whom it belongs and the obedience of the nations is his" (Gen. 49:10). This prophecy points to Jesus Christ, to whom the scepter of rule belongs. He will be granted the obedience of the nations, as Matthew confirms when quoting from Isaiah: "In his name the nations will put their hope" (Matt. 12:21). God will fulfill his worldwide plan, first of all, through Jesus.

But let's climb in just a bit more. How would he fulfill his plan through Jesus? He would do it through Jesus' atoning death, a death by which Jesus "purchased men for God from every tribe and language and people and nation," as we have already read (Rev. 5:9).

And what of these purchased people? When Peter confesses in the Gospel of Matthew that Jesus is the Messiah, the Christ, Jesus promises that he will build his church—his assembly—on Peter and Peter's confession (Matt. 16:18). Then two chapters later, Jesus gives his authority to this assembly, this church (Matt. 18:15–18). And then what does he promise his disciples at the end of Matthew? That he who had all authority in heaven and on earth would be with them always to the very end of the age, and that *they* were to go and make disciples of all nations!

How would God accomplish his plan to bring himself glory among all peoples? Through Jesus Christ, and specifically through the church of Jesus Christ. Therefore, we should not be surprised to find story after story throughout the book of Acts of Christ's followers not merely evangelizing the lost, but congregating the converted. They planted churches.

Indeed, we should also not be surprised because God had established this pattern in the Old Testament. The Lord said to his people in the wilderness through Moses, "I am the LORD your God, who has set you apart from the nations. . . . You are to be holy to me because I, the LORD, am holy, and I have set you apart from the nations to be my own" (Lev. 20:24, 26). Israel's obedience was to lead the nations to blessing and to glorying in the true God (Jer. 4:1–2). His people were the means to bring him glory.

And as in the Old, so in the New. Individual Christians bring God glory, of course. But God also intends for the church—or what Paul calls "the Israel of God" (Gal. 6:16)—to bring him glory throughout the nations through our corporate life together. That is his plan.

The Problem

But what is the problem? The problem is that God's people were unfaithful.

God's Old Testament people bore his name. He had set them in the middle of the nations, and their fame spread because of what God had given them (Ezek. 5:5; 16:14). But instead of honoring God's name and bringing him glory, they "mingled with the nations and adopted their customs. They worshiped their idols" (Ps. 106:35–36). So God judged the northern kingdom through Assyria and the southern kingdom through Babylon. While the people of Judah were in Babylon, God explained again and again that he does everything he does for the sake of his name, saying things like "for the sake of my holy name, which you have profaned among the nations . . . my great name, which has been profaned among the nations, the name you have profaned among them" (Ezek. 36:22–23; cf. 36:20; Rom. 2:24). God exiled his people so that the nations would see that he disapproved of his people's unholiness and how they misrepresented him (Ezek. 5:14–15; 16:27). They were to be light to the nations (Isa. 60:3), but they brought shame on God's name instead. Even centuries later Paul would quote from the prophets to remind his Jewish readers, "God's name is blasphemed among the Gentiles because of you" (Rom. 2:24).

This is what God does. He does everything for the glory of his name (see Ezek. 20; esp. vv. 9, 14, 22, 44; 28:25), even if it means disciplining and exiling his people. (As a side note, non-Christians hate that message, while true Christians love it.) If God seemed harder on Israel for their sins than he was on others, it was because he had set his name on them, such that their holiness was especially attached to his reputation and glory.

This same teaching echoes throughout the New Testament. So Jesus teaches his disciples, "let your light shine before men, that they may see your good deeds and praise your Father in heaven" (Matt. 5:16). The good deeds of Christians are not meant to bring praise to us, but to God since they reveal his character to his creation. Peter, likewise, writes, "Live such good lives among the pagans that, though they accuse you of doing wrong, they may see your good deeds and glorify God on the day he visits us" (1 Pet. 2:12). God has united his name to the church, and our lives bear on his reputation before the nations for good or for ill.

This brings us to the matter of church members who live worldly, carnal lives, and why it is such a significant matter. Consider the immoral church member in 1 Corinthians 5. His life represented Christ falsely.

But the larger problem I am interested in here is not just the occasional hypocrite who is lost in unrepentant sin like this Corinthian man, but with the systems and methods that can produce whole congregations of false converts such that, like Israel of old, they are characterized not by holiness but by worldliness. Do you see the dimensions of this problem? Let me mention four effects of false conversions.

1. False conversions deceive the individuals themselves about their state before the Lord. In 1 Corinthians Paul gives one reason for why the church should put the hypocritical man out of their fellowship— so that his spirit may be "saved on the day of the Lord" (5:5). It is not loving or right for a congregation to leave men and women made in the image of God with the impression that they are reconciled to God when the truth is, other than some decision recorded decades earlier, there is no evidence that they are.

2. False conversions deceive a church and hinder love within the body. Paul is worried about just one unrepentant person being left in the membership—a little yeast works through the whole batch of dough, he says (1 Cor. 5:6). What then are the implications for a church body who has not just one but many such persons, even hundreds of them? How does that change a church's life together? Does it not make the church less loving, forgiving, joyful, and hopeful?

And what toll does a large number of false converts take on its leaders? The author of Hebrews exhorts Christians to make their leaders' work a joy and not a burden (13:17). No doubt, pastors are accustomed to dealing with sin: their own, their family's, their church's. Indeed, their churches are composed exclusively of sinners! But congregations are to be composed of *born-again* sinners, *repenting* sinners. When a congregation is comprised of many people whose lives more resemble the works of the flesh than the fruit of the Spirit, the experience of following Christ together—of love, encouragement, spurring on, mutual edification, accountability—is cooled and diminished. The church becomes more like the world.

3. False conversions deceive the nations by subverting the church's witness. We become so much like the world that the world has no questions to ask us. It looks to them as if we can offer no hope of a better, more humane, more God-honoring life. When the world is in the church, the church begins to disappear from the world. We should be a light shining in darkness, but if our words are not true, or if they are not backed up by our lives, then what should be a beacon of hope and life is dimmed. The way to God seems to disappear. Hope vanishes.

4. False conversions defame the glory of God's name. God has set apart a people for himself for his own glory. But with false conversions, what was designed for his praise tends instead to the profaning, even blaspheming, of his name, just as Ezekiel warned about.

I have always been struck by how Paul dealt with divisiveness in the Corinthian church. He asks the penetrating question, "Is Christ divided?" (1 Cor. 1:13), a question with clear theological assumptions behind it: The local church should reflect the truth about God. If it is divided, it teaches everyone that Christ is divided! Paul goes on in this letter to teach that the Corinthians' holiness should reflect God's holiness, and their love should reflect God's love.

Our churches should reflect the character of God *so that* he will be brought glory in the nations! This has always been his plan. This is what he has done, is doing, and will do. But we work against him when we build churches that camouflage his character rather than display it. False conversions obscure God's plan.

The Source of the Problem

In too many congregations, a large, even dominant, number of people do not evidence the fruit of the Spirit. They do not seem to be born-again. How does this happen? What have we been doing to create such false conversions?

Often the problem lies with those of us who are pastors since our role in the church is crucial. It should not surprise us to see so many warnings about false teachers in the New Testament. So Paul warns Timothy to "have nothing to do with godless myths" (1 Tim. 4:7).

He also warns that false teachers will come and deceive many (2 Tim. 3:13). Sometimes this is what the people will ask for: "The time will come when men will not put up with sound doctrine. Instead, to suit their own desires, they will gather around them a great number of teachers to say what their itching ears want to hear" (2 Tim. 4:3).

Peter warns his readers that there will be "false prophets among the people, just as there will be false teachers among you." He continues, "In their greed these teachers will exploit you with stories they have made up" (2 Pet. 2:1, 3).

John refers to "those who are trying to lead you astray" (1 John 2:26), which is why he tells his audience to "not believe every spirit, but test the spirits to see whether they are from God, because many false prophets have gone out into the world" (1 John 4:1).

It should be plain why the role of pastor is so important. If God has a grand plan, if his people are part of that plan, and if pastors play a crucial role among his people, then you understand why teachers have such great responsibility and will be accountable for this responsibility to God. That is why James writes, "Not many of you should presume to be teachers, my brothers, because you know that we who teach will be judged more strictly" (3:1). The author of Hebrews, likewise, observes that church leaders will "give an account" to God (13:17).

All this brings us back to the text with which we began, and one that well summarizes how a pastor can work against false conversions: "Watch your life and doctrine closely. Persevere in them, because if you do, you will save both yourself and your hearers" (1 Tim. 4:16). Notice that Paul speaks to both life and doctrine since we can go wrong in either of these ways.

Watch Your Doctrine

Let's think first about the doctrine that pastors teach because it sets the tone for a church's life. If the true gospel leads to faith

(Rom. 10:17), false doctrine leads to disaster, including false converts (2 Tim. 3:13–16; e.g., the danger in Galatians). As I look through the New Testament, I see at least five related truths that are especially liable to being distorted or overlooked. And protecting God's church against false converts requires pastors to especially teach these often-attacked, easily overlooked truths:

1. Teach that God's judgment is coming. Many pastors seem to avoid the doctrine of God's judgment. Of course Peter predicted this: "First of all, you must understand that in the last days scoffers will come, scoffing and following their own evil desires. They will say, 'Where is this "coming" he promised? Ever since our fathers died, everything goes on as it has since the beginning of creation'" (2 Pet. 3:3–4).

But we pastors love our congregations by teaching them about God's judgment. And we must teach them that God's judgment is coming because God is good.

If we deny or just ignore God's role as judge of this world, then people will follow their own evil desires. And it is comparatively easy to fill a church by ignoring this truth, drawing people instead with one reason or another. But beware this temptation. Avoiding the doctrine of hell is one step away from denying it all together.

When you get this teaching right, the congregation's life will begin to be characterized by mutual care and humility. As members meditate on the brevity of life and the certainty of judgment, they will increasingly perceive themselves to be objects of mercy rather than judges, more pilgrims than settlers, more stewards than owners.

2. Teach that God should judge each one of us. At birth, every one of us is lost, depraved, and under the good, right, fearful, and certain judgment of God. This second point is much like the first, but it presses in the matter of judgment a bit more. Pastors should teach their people not merely that God will judge someone *out there.* People need to know and feel their *own* helplessness. It's not just that

God will judge, it's that God will judge *us*. Because God is good and we are not, we deserve God's judgment! Paul argues in Romans 1:32 that we "know God's righteous decree that those who do such things deserve death." And by Romans 3, Paul has shown that this includes all of us!

One part of depravity that we pastors must especially understand and consider is the natural spiritual state of people apart from grace. All people have a natural indisposition toward believing the gospel message (see Eph. 2:8–9). Men love darkness instead of light (John 3:19). Knowing and teaching this protects us from the mistake of thinking that we can get more conversions by changing the message. How many churches downplay if not deny natural human depravity and lostness? But to what purpose? We know that those who are "from the world" (1 John 4:4–6) will not accept the true gospel. If they do accept the gospel, it is not because of anything in them, but because of the power of the gospel we preach and the Spirit.

But when pastors rightly preach God's judgment as well as our deadness in sin, we protect the church against those "converts" who are offended at the idea that they have done anything wrong, let alone that God should judge them for it.

Do you see how our humility grows as we move from accepting the awesome judgment of God to accepting that this awesome judgment should fall on us? Not only that, our understanding of God's grace and the mercy that we each need deepens.

I remember once conducting a church membership interview, and in the course of the interview, the man admitted that he had questions about the eternality of God's punishment. I therefore told him not to join the church just yet, but to go and read several resources as well as a number of biblical passages on God's judgment. A couple of weeks later, he contacted me, now convinced of the eternality of God's judgment. In the course of the second interview that followed, he remarked that, through reading about God's judgment, Christ's atonement had become much sweeter to him.

3. Teach that hope is found in Christ alone. A pastor must teach very clearly that a person's hope and trust must not be in who they are or what they have done, but in Jesus Christ and what he has done—that God became man in Christ, that he died on the cross as a substitute for everyone who repents and believes, that he rose again for our justification and as the firstfruits of the final resurrection.

- So any idea that people can be converted through our own works must be rejected. Romans 1–3 by itself clearly destroys any such idea.
- We must confess that Jesus is the Christ and the incarnate Son of God (see 1 John 2:20–25; 3:23; 4:2–3, 9–10, 14–16; 5:5, 10–12).
- We must be clear not only about his person but about his atoning work. "This is how we know what love is: Jesus Christ laid down his life for us" (1 John 3:16; cf. 2:2).
- We must also be clear, over against theological liberalism, that denying the bodily resurrection of Christ, according to the Bible, is denying Christ himself. What else is Paul's majestic 1 Corinthians 15 about?!

Without preaching salvation through Christ alone, we can make converts to fatalism or to an ethical society, as so many Protestant churches have become. But we cannot have a truly Christian church.

When we get this teaching right, we both offend and attract all the right people. The self-righteous and wrongly self-confident will be offended at such talk of a Savior, while those who know they are sinners in need of a Savior will hear the news and rejoice. Only true converts finally respond to the truth about Jesus Christ.

4. Teach that Christians won't experience the fullness of salvation in this life. What I mean is, Christ's death and resurrection secure forgiveness and reconciliation with God eternally, and his sustaining Spirit until then. So it is wrong to teach that following Jesus is mainly for present, this-life benefits. Such teaching turns the great examples of faith in Hebrews 11 into nonsense. Christians must learn that, like those figures, we are aliens and strangers on earth who are "looking for a country of their own . . . [and] longing for a better country—a heavenly one" (vv. 14, 16). Authentic Christianity teaches that we are all "wait[ing] for the blessed hope—the glorious appearing of our great God and Savior, Jesus Christ" (Titus 2:13; cf. Rom. 8:24–25). And so we agree with Paul when he wrote, "If only for this life we have hope in Christ, we are to be pitied more than all men" (1 Cor. 15:19).

The earthly trials encountered by the saints in Hebrews 11 are hardly things that most people would want. But if you instead hold out a picture of Jesus as the way to reach one's fullest potential in this life, how many would then be interested? Indeed, even carnally minded people want to better their life. You can assemble vast crowds by simply promising meaning and purpose. Of course, that is not the same thing as repenting of your sins before God.

But when we pastors get these things right in our heads, hearts, and teaching, we help our congregations to fear God more than the king's anger and to accept disgrace for the sake of Christ. We help them to see that Christ is worth more than all earthly treasure. We help them to trust all of God's commands, even when they would seem to jeopardize our hopes in this life. Indeed, teaching churches to prize Christ above all becomes a powerful engine for encouraging self-sacrifice.

5. *Teach how easy it is to deceive ourselves and others about our relationship with God.* If you do not want your church to be characterized by an unconverted worldliness, then you must regularly remind the church of how easily fallen human beings—saved or unsaved—can deceive themselves. The idea that everyone who thinks they are a

Christian is a Christian is a false and dangerous idea. It populates our churches with those who are spiritually dead. The spiritually dead can get excited about some of the activities and programs that churches offer. But such interest is no evidence of the life of the Spirit or reconciliation with God. That is why Paul exhorted the Corinthians, "Examine yourselves to see whether you are in the faith; test yourselves" (2 Cor. 13:5). If you are a pastor, it is worth asking yourself: Would the people in your church understand what those words mean? Would they understand why possessing godly "qualities in increasing measure" would help to make your calling and election sure, as Peter teaches (2 Pet. 1:3–10)?

When a congregation gets this point right, it grows in humble joy, a sharpened understanding of God's grace, and a child-like reliance on him.

Again, if you are a pastor, think about the people that you have baptized in this last year. Did you clearly teach them these five things? Do they believe them? Failing to teach these five things can result in many false professions.

False teachers create false converts, and false converts hire false teachers (e.g., Jude 3–4, 17–23). There is a symbiotic relationship. The Lord Jesus said this was one of the problems in the church at Thyatira (Rev. 2:20–24). They tolerated false teachers who, in turn, misled them. So if you want to make sure that your successor does not preach the gospel, just admit many people into membership who are not truly converted.

Remember what 1 Timothy 4:16 says: "Watch your life and doctrine closely. Persevere in them, because if you do, you will save both yourself and your hearers." Paul exhorts Timothy to watch his doctrine closely, for the sake of the souls of those who hear him.

Watch Your Life

But Paul also exhorts Timothy to watch his life closely. Wrong living can be as damning as wrong teaching. The book of James, for instance, is very clear: we can be hearers and believers and yet not doers and workers and livers. And fruit-less, works-less, deed-less faith is no true faith. It is dead. It will never save.

So we pastors must give attention to our lives. Those who listen to us also watch us. As imperfect people, we will always be open to careless charges of hypocrisy when preaching the truth. Still, our lives should back up our sermons.

Yet not only is the life of the pastor important, the life of the whole congregation is.

The early churches suffered from three common errors that still plague us, and who knows how many people are deceived by such errors?

1. It is an error to present a church without holiness. Christ has called his church to be holy as he is holy. Sadly, unholiness thrives in the churches where their pastors ignorantly avoid teaching on sin, fearing that it will undermine grace. And unholiness thrives in churches where there is no accountability between members, because the churches were built to cater to our culture's individualism and commitment to privacy. But in the New Testament, the Christian life is motivated by a love of God that is contrary to the love of this world, a love that is holy.

Again, John offers protection for us here. He teaches that "If we claim to have fellowship with [God] yet walk in the darkness, we lie and do not live by the truth" (1 John 1:6; cf. 2:15–17, 29; 3:3, 6–10, 23–24; Rev. 2:20–24). I wonder, is your church clear in their understanding of this? Or do people in you congregation feel like they can walk in darkness and still be affirmed as having fellowship with God? John says elsewhere, "The man who says, 'I know him,' but does not do what he commands is a liar, and the truth is not in him" (1 John 2:4). And still elsewhere: "This is love for God: to obey his commands" (1 John 5:3).

The author of Hebrews likewise writes, "Without holiness no one will see the Lord" (Heb. 12:14).

Paul, too, lists a number of sins that the Corinthians may have been tempted to think they could continue indulging and still inherit the kingdom of God, but he warns them that such an idea was deception (see 1 Cor. 6:9–11). Instead, churches should use the two lists he provides in Galatians 5 of the works of the flesh and the fruit of the Spirit to compare our lives against. Otherwise, we are prone to deceive ourselves concerning holiness. Christians should belong to churches, among other reasons, to wake us up from self-deception. Left to ourselves, we too easily fall into a spiritual slumber, which is to our undoing forever (like the man in 1 Corinthians 5).

How tempting it is for a church to call itself grace-giving, and then to tolerate all sin, not asking its people to repent. But the truth is, a church growing in holiness by the power of the Spirit is a church growing in beauty, health, and freedom. God's Spirit helps us to begin living the lives for which we were made to live. We become morally visible to one another within the church, and then, as a community, we reflect God's character and likeness more and more!

2. It is an error to present a church without suffering. This is temptation to all of us. Left to ourselves we would all avoid poverty and sickness, which, in one sense, is a fine goal for our lives and work. But such goals are too small for biblical Christianity. If we espouse them we will mislead others about what Christ saves us from. He saves us from ultimate moral bankruptcy and death, not necessarily from suffering in this world.

Indeed, true Christianity calls us to suffering. Most of us recognize that "Health and Wealth" preachers are false teachers. But do we teach the same thing, albeit in more mild ways? It is common to find churches that practice a subtle triumphalism in everything from the smiling faces, to the music, to the whole atmosphere, a triumphalism which boasts that everything is great. Carl Trueman was onto something when, several years ago, he titled an excellent article, "What Can Miserable Christians Sing?" He wondered whether our churches would make room for the lament of the Psalms in our gatherings.

Suffering is a prominent theme in Peter's first letter. In chapter 2, we are told that "Christ suffered for you, leaving you an example, that you should follow in his steps" (v. 21). In chapter 3, we learn that "It is better, if it is God's will, to suffer for doing good than for doing evil" (v. 17). Or chapter 4: "If you suffer as a Christian, do not be ashamed, but praise God that you bear that name. . . . So then, those who suffer according to God's will should commit themselves to their faithful Creator and continue to do good" (vv. 16, 19).

If you want to get a lot of fake Christians in your church, just tell them that God offers a free gift that entails no self-sacrifice, and that the Bible's talk about "trouble" and "taking up a cross" is only for the super saints.

The truth, however, is no cross, no crown. Jesus promised his disciples that "In this world you will have trouble" (John 16:33; cf. Mark 4:17; 1 John 3:13). And he told those who were considering following him, "If anyone would come after me, he must deny himself and take up his cross and follow me" (Mark 8:34).

What wonderful life can be found in our churches, what truth and goodness, when we realistically acknowledge the fallenness and darkness of our hearts and this world, and then oppose this darkness with God's strength.

3. It is an error to present a church without love. Your church can affirm all the right doctrines, and even possess a grim willingness to suffer. But if love does not mark your church, then it may attract spiritual hobbyists and theological accountants who like to play at religion and theology, but not people of real Christian love who inconvenience themselves for others. We must beware the temptation to dry orthodoxy which mouths spiritual truths from dead hearts.

The connection between real Christianity and love for fellow Christians runs through John's first letter. In chapter 1, John teaches us, "if we walk in the light . . . we have fellowship with one another" (1:7; cf. 2:5–6; 3:23; 4:16–17). In chapter 2, he observes, "Anyone who claims to be in the light but hates his brother is still in the darkness" (v. 9). In chapter 3, he teaches that such love is a distinguishing mark of those who are truly converted: "We know that we have passed from death to life, because we love our brothers. Anyone who does not love remains in death" (v. 14). Chapter 4, too: "Whoever does not love does not know God, because God is love" (v. 8). And if that is true, we morally ought to love: "Dear friends, since God so loved us, we also ought to love one another" (v. 11). Indeed, the presence of love for our fellow believers is a test of whether or not we love God: "We love because he first loved us. If anyone says, 'I love God,' yet hates his brother, he is a liar. For anyone who does not love his brother, whom he has seen, cannot love God, whom he has not seen. And he has given us this command: Whoever loves God must also love his brother" (1 John 4:19–21).

Have you experienced life in a Christian congregation that is suffused with love? Where people initiate care, empathize in grief, cook meals, give rides, overlook offenses, express affection, offer help, extend forgiveness, share joy? One of our world's most striking needs is churches full of true Christians who give themselves away to each other and to others in love. The world celebrates cheap imitations and partial renditions of true love. But to experience real Christian love—which comes with authority, kindness, correction, self-sacrifice, and wisdom—is bracing, even shocking. True, many are repelled by such love. But it's also true that, by God's grace, many will be attracted by this message of the self-giving love of God in Christ.

Conclusion: Practical Suggestions

Is it clear that false conversions are the suicide of the local church?

The last thing I want to share are a few practical suggestions on how a pastor can help to prevent this from characterizing your church, or help to change it if it has. Three simple encouragements:

1. Always be evangelizing, and evangelize steadily and well.

I quote from Spurgeon's book, *The Soul Winner*:

> Remember our Saviour's words, "The kingdom of heaven is like unto a net, that was cast into the sea, and gathered of every kind: which, when it was full, they drew to shore, and sat down, and gathered the good into vessels, but cast the bad away." Do not number your fishes before they are broiled, nor count your converts before you have tested and tried them. This process may make your work somewhat slow, but then, brethren, it will be sure. Do your work steadily and well, so that those who come after you may not have to say that it was far more trouble to them to clear the church of those who ought never to have been admitted than it was to you to admit them.[2]

Ask yourself what temptations you face to evangelize in such manner that would create a large proportion of false converts. Be wary of the "bigger is better" culture in your church. Don't mistake a device of the enemy for the work of God. Greater numbers do not necessarily mean greater strength.

2. Always shepherd sheep.

Re-center your thoughts as a pastor on the individuals to be shepherded. How you pastor individual sheep will vary depending on whether your church is comprised of 17 people or 70 or 700 or 7,000, but remember that when you take someone into membership, you are telling them that they give good evidence of being born again, that they are eternally fine! Now, this is a wonderful role that churches and pastors have. Again, if I can turn to Mr. Spurgeon:

> I am occupied in my small way, as Mr. Great-heart was employed in Bunyan's day. I do not compare myself with that champion, but I am in the same line of business. I am engaged in personally-conducted tours to Heaven; and I have with me, at the present time, dear Old Father Honest: I am glad he is still alive and active. And there is Christiana, and there are her children. It is my business, as best I can, to kill dragons, and cut off giants' heads, and lead on the timid and trembling. I am often afraid of losing some of the weaklings. I have the heartache for them; but, by God's grace, and your kind and generous help in looking after one another, I hope we shall all travel safely to the river's edge. Oh, how many have I had to part with there! I have stood on the brink, and I have heard them singing in the midst of the stream, and I have almost seen the shining ones lead them up the hill, and through the gates, into the Celestial City.[3]

By the way, this is why membership and discipline are so important. If you are reforming a church, you should not merely "clean the roles" to get more accurate numbers. Each one of those numbers is an individual made in the image of God that your church has told is reconciled with God, now and forever! These unaccounted for members are a field of ministry and a responsibility.

I am also reminded of the significance of each individual through personal evangelism, sharing testimonies, membership interviews, praying through our church's membership directory, even standing around after a service to talk to people.

3. Always remember the account that you will give to God.

Our great accountability to God makes sense when we remember the great plan that God has, and the crucial role of the church in that plan. Pastors will give an account to God for how they pastor the sheep. In his letter of paternal counsel to one of his pupils newly ordained over a small congregation, John Brown wrote:

> I know the vanity of your heart, and that you will feel mortified that your congregation is very small, in comparison with those of your brethren around you; but assure yourself on the word of an old man, that when you come to give an account of them to the Lord Christ, at his judgment-seat, you will think you have had enough.[4]

Back to 1 Timothy 4:16: "Watch your life and doctrine closely. Persevere in them, because if you do, you will save both yourself and your hearers."

Did you notice he mentioned saving yourself? We preachers can be lost. Perhaps you've heard of Gilbert Tennant's famous message preached in 1740 on "The Danger of an Unconverted Ministry." Spurgeon said it best: "God never saved any man for being a preacher."[5]

Testimony: William "Trip Lee" Barefield III

My name is Trip.

I have never been drunk, never done drugs, and never lived a wild lifestyle. But I was hopelessly dead in my sins. I grew up in the Bible Belt and was very confused about what it actually meant to be a Christian. Everybody around me professed to know Christ, but there was nothing distinct about most of their lifestyles.

When I was five or six, I repeated a prayer after a children's pastor and thought this made me a Christian. When I look back, though, I don't think I was reborn because my sin did not bother me and Jesus was not precious to me. But I went on professing Christ with my lips, and spitting in his face with my lifestyle. I was a pretty good kid by most standards, but I was self-absorbed and far from God.

When I was around thirteen years old, I started to get involved in a youth group, mainly for social reasons. But by God's grace, the youth pastor was faithful to preach the Word, and God began to open my eyes. Different aspects of the gospel started to click. I began to understand God's holiness and my sin, and then my separation from God and what Christ did for me on the cross. Around age fourteen I went to an event with the youth group where a preacher called people to repentance. In that moment all the gospel truth I had begun to understand weighed on my heart. God opened my eyes, and moved me to repent and trust in Jesus.

After that my entire world looked different. The Lord gave me an incredible desire to know him in his Word, and he began to change my life. I remember when I first began to read the Bible. I read a passage one night, and the very next day I was faced with a situation where that Scripture applied. I was blown away! I couldn't believe that this old book actually had power to transform my life here and now.

God has sent numerous godly men into my life over the years to teach me the Word and to help me better follow Christ. And he has graciously allowed me to become a minister of the same truth he used to rescue me.

I could easily still be deceived about my relationship with God, but the Good News about Jesus rocked me and opened my eyes. Don't underestimate the power of the gospel.

6

WHEN A PASTOR LOSES HEART

C. J. Mahaney

Scripture quotations in this chapter are from ESV.

"Pray that I would not bomb so often when I preach," said my friend after I inquired how I could pray for him.

My pen froze. I looked up, incredulous. I could not bring myself to write it down. But the expression on his face was serious; he was not joking. He wanted me to ask God that he not bomb so often when he preaches.

Mind you, this was not a seminary student in his first homiletics class or a rookie church planter halfway through his first sermon series. This friend is one of the best preachers I know. His name is instantly recognizable, since he is one of the most gifted expositors of our time. I demanded a different prayer request.

We left dinner and drove to the conference we were attending where my friend proceeded to preach an exceptional message. As he descended from the platform, I congratulated him: "Hey! You didn't bomb!"

But later, as we navigated the parking lot, my friend began to lament that he *had* bombed once again. I sought to encourage him, but his countenance remained downcast. I reviewed with him all the ways I benefitted from his sermon: his model exegesis, his memorable illustrations, his pointed application. None of it seemed to resonate. I reached deep into my bag of encouragement options: "My friend, surely you noticed that no one coughed. That was a cough-free sermon!" When even this line of encouragement failed to restore my friend from his post-preaching malaise, I was forced to resort to my old fallback: name-calling.

"You are an idiot."

Have You Lost Heart?

Later that evening, I reflected on this episode. While my friend is unique in his preaching gift, international influence, and writing ministry, he is not unique in his temptation to discouragement. In fact, no pastor is exempt from this temptation. I cannot help but wonder how many pastors who hoist this book do so because they are looking for something heartening. Maybe you have lost heart. Perhaps in the last few months, or few years, you have found your passion for pastoral ministry waning. Maybe you have remained faithful and even fruitful in your ministry, but you are no longer joyful.

What pastor doesn't spend Monday (as well as Sunday afternoon and maybe Tuesday too) mentally reviewing and evaluating the sermon and the service? This is a useful barometer for a pastor's heart: How are your Mondays? Do you find yourself regularly rejoicing in the privilege to serve God's people, or discouraged over what you perceive to be a lack of effectiveness in ministry? The temptation to lose heart pulses predictably each week, does it not?

Friends, we are not alone as we confront this temptation. And while we may find it somewhat heartening that other pastors can relate, there is one pastor in particular whose experience can provide us with singular and significant encouragement. I am referring to the apostle Paul. In his second letter to the Corinthian church he describes his temptation to lose heart.

I am not sure there is a more important letter for pastors to study than 2 Corinthians. And there is no more important chapter for pastors in 2 Corinthians than chapter 4. Here Paul reveals his own temptation to lose heart—but he also provides a remedy for this pastoral malady. Read 2 Corinthians chapter 4 slowly and notice how Paul begins and ends with his resolve to not lose heart.

> Therefore, having this ministry by the mercy of God, *we do not lose heart*. But we have renounced disgraceful, underhanded ways. We refuse to practice cunning or to tamper with God's word, but by the open statement of the truth we would commend ourselves to everyone's conscience in the sight of God. And even if our gospel is veiled, it is veiled only to those who are perishing. In their case the god of this world has blinded the minds of the unbelievers, to keep them from seeing the light of the gospel of the glory of Christ, who is the image of God. For what we proclaim is not ourselves, but Jesus Christ as Lord, with ourselves as your servants for Jesus' sake. For God, who said, "Let light shine out of darkness," has shone in our hearts to give the light of the knowledge of the glory of God in the face of Jesus Christ.
>
> But we have this treasure in jars of clay, to show that the surpassing power belongs to God and not to us. We are afflicted in every way, but not crushed; perplexed, but not driven to despair; persecuted, but

not forsaken; struck down, but not destroyed; always
carrying in the body the death of Jesus, so that the
life of Jesus may also be manifested in our bodies.
For we who live are always being given over to death
for Jesus' sake, so that the life of Jesus also may be
manifested in our mortal flesh. So death is at work
in us, but life in you.

Since we have the same spirit of faith according to what has been written, "I believed, and so I
spoke," we also believe, and so we also speak, knowing that he who raised the Lord Jesus will raise
us also with Jesus and bring us with you into his
presence. For it is all for your sake, so that as grace
extends to more and more people it may increase
thanksgiving, to the glory of God.

So we do not lose heart. Though our outer self is
wasting away, our inner self is being renewed day by
day. For this light momentary affliction is preparing
for us an eternal weight of glory beyond all comparison, as we look not to the things that are seen but
to the things that are unseen. For the things that are
seen are transient, but the things that are unseen are
eternal. (emphasis added)

"We do not lose heart." We encounter this phrase at the outset
of chapter 4 and it appears again in verse 16. Apparently, Paul was
very familiar with this temptation to lose heart in the midst of the
challenges and opposition that he encountered as he proclaimed the
gospel, planted churches, and cared for pastors. In chapter 11, he
concludes his extensive list of trials and suffering and hardship by
referring to the daily pressure of anxiety he feels for all the churches.
This was a man who was no stranger to the temptation to lose heart,

and particularly with the Corinthian church, given his intense and difficult relationship with them.

In light of all he suffered, in light of all the responsibility he carried, in light of all the opposition he endured, these are remarkable statements. *Though tempted to lose heart, he resolved by the grace of God not to lose heart.*

Whether we are in the depths of Monday melancholy or we are currently heartened for the ministry to which we have been called, we can all learn from Paul's resolve to not lose heart. What informed his resolve? How can we follow his example? What does a pastor do when he begins to lose heart for his role and task? In chapter 4 Paul provides us with three heart-protecting, heart-strengthening realities for the disheartened pastor.

1. The Call of Christian Ministry

No pastor will long retain a heart for the ministry if he loses sight of his call to the ministry. Paul's awareness of the nature and purpose of his call strengthened and protected him from joyless ministry.

Paul references this call in verse 1 with the phrase, "having this ministry." Then in rapid-fire succession, he describes the nature of this call. In verse 2: "the open statement of the truth." Verse 3: "our gospel." Verse 4: "the gospel of the glory of Christ." And finally verse 5: "what we proclaim is not ourselves, but Jesus Christ as Lord." Paul's ministry—like every pastor's ministry—was a call to proclaim the gospel of Jesus Christ and him crucified. It was a ministry of proclamation. And it was the call to "this ministry" that strengthened Paul's resolve to not lose heart.

Paul's personal history with the Corinthian church provides a vivid example of how the Lord strengthens a pastor's heart by reminding him of his call to "this ministry" of proclamation. This made all the difference for Paul when he originally arrived in Corinth and experienced opposition to his preaching of the gospel. When he was tempted to lose heart, the Lord revealed himself one night in a vision and said to him, "Do not be afraid, but go on speaking and do not be silent, for I am with you, and no one will attack you to harm you, for I have many in this city who are my people" (Acts 18:9–10).

And so Paul did not lose heart. He remained in Corinth so that through his preaching those whom God had chosen would come to faith. The Corinthian church was created by the grace of God, through Paul's ministry of gospel proclamation. In effect, the Corinthians became a living illustration of verses 4 through 6. And the glorious nature and effect of this call to proclaim the gospel sustained Paul in ministry.

Though Paul's call and ministry were certainly unique, we too have been called to "this ministry." As we declare the truth of the gospel to those who have been blinded by the god of this world, the same God who dispelled darkness at creation will dispel the darkness of their heart. And what a sight they will see: the light of the knowledge of the glory of God in the face of Jesus Christ. As we proclaim *him*, God gives sight to *them*. Pastoral ministry is an ongoing confrontation with the god of this world, with blindness, with hardness of heart, and with remaining sin. But we do not lose heart, because we have been called to "this ministry" to proclaim this message of the gospel that gives light, reveals glory, and transforms lives.

And because we are called to preach this message, we must do so with integrity, as defined in verse 2: "We refuse to practice cunning or tamper with God's word." This message must not be tampered with or altered in any way, and we must resist any impulse to do so. Those who tamper with or try to add to this message underestimate it. We are not innovators. We are proclaimers.

Not only are we proclaimers, we are proclaimers *of a particular message*. We do not proclaim ourselves, but Jesus Christ as Lord (v. 5). We don't preach to draw attention to ourselves. We preach to draw attention to him. After being captured and captivated by the light of the knowledge of the glory of God in the face of Jesus Christ, who would want to preach about themselves? If you have been called to "this ministry," you will desire to proclaim *him*, to please *him*, and to live aware that your call is purely by the mercy of God.

The mercy of God is where Paul begins. Look again at verse one: "Therefore, having this ministry by the mercy of God . . ." Paul's resolve to not lose heart was informed by his awareness of the mercy of God in his conversion and call to ministry. He never stopped marveling at the mercy of God. Some thirty years after his conversion, Paul wrote to Timothy, "Though formerly I was a blasphemer, a persecutor, and insolent opponent. But I received mercy" (1 Tim. 1:13). He never lost sight of mercy in his conversion and call to ministry so that he would never lose heart.

How about you? Have you lost sight of mercy? Have you gotten over it or become familiar with it? Are you still amazed? No doubt there was a time when you were very conscious that your call to "this ministry" is because of the mercy of God. Do you continue to live like Paul with this keen sense of the mercy of God in your life?

If you have lost sight of mercy and lost heart in ministry, let's take a moment for a heart-strengthening review of how we got here. Though different in the details, I know that your story follows the same basic trajectory as mine. In light of my sinfulness and God's holiness, the only explanation for receiving this call to "this ministry" to preach the gospel is the mercy of God. Every day, there is sinful stuff that takes place in my heart. Every day, I fall short of my calling as a Christian and a minister of God's Word. I am not worthy of this task of proclamation. In fact, I am decidedly unworthy. But because of God's mercy, I have been entrusted with this gospel and called to preach the gospel.

And when I do preach the gospel, God, in his marvelous mercy, dispels the darkness that captivates hearts because of sin and Satan. Because of his mercy, God gives sight to the blind. They see that bleeding sacrifice. They hear the cries of Calvary. They perceive his sacrifice as for them. They recognize him as their sin-bearing, wrath-absorbing substitute. They acknowledge Jesus as the one the Father raised from the dead, satisfied with his perfect life and substitutionary sacrifice. When sinners see these glorious truths, they turn from their sin and trust in the Savior for the forgiveness of sin and their lives are transformed. By the mercy of God, we have the privilege to proclaim this message. Friend, if you are discouraged in ministry, remember this!

We see the transforming effect of God's mercy in verses 4 through 6. If we only had verse 4, the situation would indeed be hopeless: "In their case the god of this world has blinded the minds of the unbelievers, to keep them from seeing the light of the gospel of the glory of Christ, who is the image of God." But look at verse 6: "For God, who said, 'Let light shine out of darkness,' has shone in our hearts to give the light of the knowledge of the glory of God in the face of Jesus Christ." From hopeless to glorious! God does what only he can do. And he brings this about through verse 5: "For what we proclaim is not ourselves, but Jesus Christ as Lord, with ourselves as your servants for Jesus' sake."

Pastor, you are in verse 5. Do you see your face there? Do you see the mercy of God at work through "this ministry"? Through *your* ministry? The apparently hopeless individual experiences this creative act of God through the means of your proclamation of the gospel. The person whom "the god of this world has blinded" sees the light of the glory of God when you proclaim the truth about Jesus Christ. Here is powerful encouragement for every discouraged pastor. Keep this in view, and you won't lose heart.

How do we put these verses to work in our soul? Quite simply, we resolve to think about our congregation in light of the truth contained here. As pastors, it is too easy for us to become preoccupied with the sins of those we serve. We can forget their conversion and lose sight of that moment when this creative act of God took place. All of this tempts us to lose heart, to become impatient and irritated. That is why we must constantly remind ourselves of the work of grace in their lives. We must recall the moment when they turned from their sins and trusted in the Savior for the forgiveness of sins.

God recently sent someone to me to help me to keep this in view. It was a friend of mine who was converted through my preaching. Every year, this friend has been faithful to send me an e-mail on the anniversary of the day he was converted. This year, he wanted to do more than send an e-mail. He wanted to meet with me and say, "Thanks again." So in the midst of all that could have preoccupied my time and attention, all the difficulties and challenges related to pastoral ministry, I found myself sitting across from this friend. And as he described his experience of conversion to me again—his transition from verse four to verse six through my proclamation of verse five—his smile filled the room. He thanked me again for preaching the gospel and told me again of the difference it has made in his life. I went back to work that day with a fresh heart for the work, amazed at the privilege I have been entrusted with to proclaim the gospel.

Brothers, may we never lose this wonder. May we never lose the sense of wonder that we have been called to pastoral ministry, the wonder that we have been called to proclaim Jesus Christ and him crucified, the wonder and marvel at the fruit of preaching the gospel.

This was one way Paul resolved to not lose heart: by remembering that he had been called to "this ministry" by the mercy of God. But it wasn't the only way. For not only was Paul called to the ministry of proclamation, he was also called to a ministry of suffering.

2. The Context of Christian Ministry

Paul marveled at being called to "this ministry," but he harbored no illusions that it would be easy. His resolve to not lose heart was informed and strengthened because he understood the context of pastoral ministry. We see this in 2 Corinthians 4:7–15; Paul understood that he was called not only to proclaim, but also to suffer and to serve.

This glorious ministry of proclamation takes place in the context of weakness and adversity. In verse 7 Paul references personal weakness and then in verses 8 and 9 he details some of the harsh realities of ministry in a fallen world: affliction, bewilderment, persecution, being struck down.

These are the harsh realities of Paul's ministry experience, not abstract hypotheticals. Paul had vivid illustrations of each of these from his own life and he provides more details in both chapter 6 and chapter 11. While Paul's suffering was unique to his calling as an apostle, our ministry in this fallen world will, by definition, involve trials, suffering, opposition, and persecution.

If you are a young or aspiring pastor, I want to help you prepare for this. Too often, too many begin in pastoral ministry aware of the mercy of God and confident in the gospel, but unprepared for the suffering that awaits them.

It is too easy to assume that verses 7 through 15 apply to Paul and not to you. But glance again, and I think you'll see your face in the photograph of these verses, for all those called to pastoral ministry appear in this picture of the Christian life. Even though Paul's call and suffering were unique, we who are called to proclaim the gospel do so in the same fallen world. And "the god of this world" is opposed to the advance of the gospel. So in every place where there is genuine gospel proclamation taking place it will always be accompanied by some degree of opposition, persecution, and suffering. No pastor is exempt from this; but it is possible for a pastor to be unprepared.

My friend, you must have your own theology of suffering firmly in place prior to your experience of verses eight and nine or else you will be blindsided. "This ministry" isn't just about proclamation. It also involves suffering. Don't be caught unawares.

Wise pastors of all ages—but especially young pastors—will carefully consider these categories. Let them inform your interaction with more seasoned saints. Ask an older pastor: "How have you experienced affliction? How have you been bewildered? How have you been persecuted? How have you been struck down? And how do you respond in a God-glorifying way?" Learn from those with more pastoral experience, and let them help you prepare for suffering.

Young pastors need to learn these lessons because *every* pastor will experience affliction in different ways and to different degrees. What is your affliction? Perhaps it is chronic illness. Perhaps it is rejection by family members because of your commitment to Christ. Perhaps it is an economic hardship from the geographic location where you have been called to serve. It is probably whatever you are thinking about as you read through these categories.

Every pastor knows what it is like to be perplexed or bewildered. It is easy to come up with hypothetical but likely scenarios. Imagine, for example, that a much-loved member of your congregation dies in a car accident. He was a godly father of three, only twenty-nine years old. As you return home from conducting the funeral, you encounter your next-door neighbor. He is an ungodly individual, consumed with worldliness and selfishness. He is aging and prospering. So why is he enjoying a long and prosperous life while your friend's widow and three small children are facing a future without a husband and father? No doubt, people in your church are looking to you for answers: "Why was this man taken from us?" But you are bewildered as well.

Or maybe, you go to the hospital to celebrate the birth of a child to a new family in your church. That weekend you conduct the funeral for that child. In a matter of days you have gone from rejoicing with that family to mourning with that family. And you are bewildered. Or it could be that for you, the bewilderment is even closer to home. Perhaps you have three kids. Two are converted; one is not. How did this happen? You preached the same gospel to them, and parented in a similar way. And now two of your children love the Lord, but one loves the world. You are bewildered. Frankly, I am so glad Paul was bewildered. I am so glad Paul understood what it was like to be perplexed and did not hesitate to tell us that this was his experience. It serves my soul to know that even the apostle Paul was sometimes stumped by his experience in ministry.

Paul wasn't only perplexed; he was also persecuted. Persecution is more subtle in this country, but it is present. Perhaps an article appears in your local paper misrepresenting you and the church. Perhaps in your county, churches are banned from using school facilities. Maybe you minister in a community where there is some form of hostility to the gospel. Pastors experience opposition and even persecution because of our proclamation of Christ. And as I write, I am aware that many of our brother-pastors around the world are faithfully and boldly leading their churches, and proclaiming the gospel in the midst of severe persecution and suffering. May this passage remind us to pray that God would give these men strength to not lose heart.

And what pastor isn't familiar with being struck down? You may not have been stoned like Paul in Lystra, but every pastor knows what it is like to be struck down in his soul. Maybe it is a friend from your preconversion days: a friend who was converted around the same time as you, helped you plant the church, and has served with you for years. Maybe that friend abruptly leaves the church, slandering you as he goes. You are struck down in your soul.

I think the most common form of being struck down for pastors is depression. Even some of the best and most well-known pastors through church history were familiar with this temptation, one of the most notable being my historical hero, Charles Spurgeon. This is why I think Spurgeon's book *Lectures to My Students* should be required reading for all pastors. If you don't have the book, I would encourage you to buy it immediately and turn to the chapter entitled "The Minister's Fainting Fits."

Charles Spurgeon knew what it was like to be struck down in his soul: "As it is recorded that David in the heat of battle waxed faint, so may it be written of all the servants of the Lord, all of them. Fits of depression come over the most of us. Usually cheerful as we may be, we must at intervals be cast down."[1]

Yes we must! This is not a possibility but a certainty. We will be cast down.

Spurgeon goes on in this chapter to explore possible reasons for pastoral depression, such as physical maladies. He then moves on to mental maladies, wondering, with a twinkle in his eye no doubt, "Is any man altogether sane? Are we not all a little off the balance?"[2] But, as Spurgeon observes, there are some people who are more vulnerable to being struck down than others: "Some minds appear to have a gloomy tinge to their very individuality."[3]

Regardless of our individual tendencies, the prince of preachers provides wise pastoral counsel for us all:

> The lesson of wisdom is to be not dismayed by soul trouble. Count it no strange thing but a part of ordinary ministerial experience. Should the power of depression be more than ordinary, think not that all is over with your usefulness. Cast not away your confidence. For it has great recompense of reward. Even if the enemy's foot be on your neck, expect to rise and overthrow him. Cast the burden of the present along with the sin of the past and the fear of the future upon the Lord who forsaketh not his saints. Live by the day, aye, by the hour. Be content to be nothing for that is what you are. And when

> your own emptiness is painfully forced upon your
> consciousness, chide yourself that you ever dreamed
> of being full except in the Lord. Set small store by
> present rewards. Be grateful for earnest by the way,
> but look of the recompensing joy here after. Between
> this and heaven, there may be rougher weather
> yet. But it is all provided for by our covenant head.
> Come fair or come foul, the pulpit is our watchtower
> and the ministry our warfare. Be it ours when we
> cannot see the face of our God to trust under the
> shadows of his wings.[4]

Friend, count it "no strange thing" when you encounter depression. It is not more than ordinary. Do not think that all is over with your usefulness. Whether you are persecuted for the sake of the gospel, or struck down in your soul, be not dismayed but "cast the burden of the present along with the sin of the past and the fear of the future upon the Lord who forsaketh not his saints."[5]

If you pursue pastoral ministry, you will encounter these harsh realities of bewilderment, persecution, and being struck down. And be warned: it isn't like they take turns. You will more than likely experience them all at the same time. You can be afflicted, bewildered, persecuted, and struck down all in a weekend. They seem to run in packs!

But these harsh realities aren't accidental or meaningless. They have a divine design. They are all purposeful. *Every experience of weakness and suffering is an opportunity for God to display his grace and glorify himself in our lives.*

That's the point of verse 7: that the surpassing power of his grace belongs to God and not to us. His power is demonstrated most fully in the midst of our weakness. In the midst of affliction and bewilderment and persecution and being struck down, here is what we discover: we discover that God is wonderfully at work. Oh, what a happy discovery this is!

Not only do we discover that God is wonderfully at work, but so does our congregation. Listen: your congregation learns from you by more than just listening to your sermons. They are studying your life as well. If you never suffered, if you were never acquainted with your weakness, they wouldn't be able to observe the power of God in your life. Your congregation is studying you all the time, but particularly when you are suffering. They want to see if the gospel makes a discernible difference in your life. They want to see if you trust God. They want to see if you remain charitable and cheerful. They want to see if you endure and don't lose heart.

While we all encounter the harsh realities described in verses 8 and 8, notice that the accent in these verses is not on the harsh realities, but on the grace of God. Read these verses again and notice the recurring refrain: *"But not . . ."*

"We are afflicted in every way, *but not* crushed; perplexed, *but not* driven to despair; persecuted, *but not* forsaken; struck down, *but not* destroyed." Do you see how the accent in this passage is on the *but not*? Paul is certainly acknowledging the harsh realities of pastoring in a fallen world. He wants us prepared for the harsh realities, but he is actually drawing attention to and celebrating the grace of God that preserves us as we encounter the harsh realities. He is celebrating the grace of God that sustains us in the midst of these harsh realities. And this brings great strength to our souls when we are tempted to lose heart.

See, ultimately, these verses are not about Paul's resolve. He is not focusing on my resolve or your resolve. The point isn't that Paul had an unusually strong constitution. Neither do you or I. Ultimately these verses are about the power of the sustaining grace of God, because left to myself I would be crushed. Left to myself I would be despairing. Left to myself I would be forsaken. Left to myself I would be destroyed. *But not . . .*

The only explanation for why we are not crushed, despairing, forsaken, or destroyed under the weight of ministry trials is because of the sustaining grace of God. It is not our resolve, but his grace that preserves us in every perplexing, discouraging, experience of suffering so that we do not lose heart.

A pastor's wife needs to be as certain of this truth as her husband—for the sake of her own soul and so that she can be best positioned to help you when you are struck down. As a pastor, there have been many times when I have been struck down. And over the years, my wife, Carolyn, has encouraged me, challenged me, and sought to bring a biblical perspective to my suffering. Sometimes her words help me immediately, bringing me right back to faith-filled joy. Other times, I have remained unresponsive for a time, and Carolyn has learned to speak the truth to me and then to wait patiently for the Lord to do this work in my soul. She is confident there will be a *but not* moment soon. Sometimes it is a matter of minutes, sometimes hours, sometimes days, but she knows *but not* is going to happen in her husband's life, because of the grace of God promised in 2 Corinthians 4.

Every pastor has *but not* written over his life. Do you see it? Does your wife see it?

As we walk though these afflictions and bewilderments, persecution, and being struck down, we must return often to these two grace-stuffed words: "but not." It is then we will discover that there is treasure in trial.

For in verses 10 through 12 Paul describes a great paradox of ministry. Mark Twain has famously said, "Most people are bothered by those passages in Scripture which they cannot understand. But as for me I have always noticed that the passages in Scripture which trouble me most are those I do understand." This is one of those passages for me. I find myself troubled by these verses because they show me that this ministry not only involves a call to proclaim the gospel, but also involves the sanctifying work of the gospel in our lives as we experience hardship, persecution, trial, and suffering.

> [We are] always carrying in the body the death of Jesus, so that the life of Jesus may also be manifested in our bodies. For we who live are always being given over to death for Jesus' sake, so that the life of Jesus also may be manifested in our mortal flesh. So death is at work in us, but life in you. (2 Cor. 4:10–12)

Murray Harris says it well: pastors are "always dying, but never lifeless." So, verse 12, "death is at work in us." Pastors are called to proclaim and to perish. Sometimes they proclaim the most through their perishing. Some of the dying we experience is mundane, like weekly sermon preparation. There you are preparing a sermon on Saturday when you want to watch the Masters. Or it is a beautiful fall day and everybody is outside making memories, having a great time. Or you have to leave early from the wedding reception to finish the message. You must prepare. You must study. You must die. Pastor's wife, you must die each and every time you give up your husband for the sake of that sermon preparation, or for that late-night hospital visit, or for that early-morning discipleship breakfast.

Some of the dying is more significant, like accepting a call to ministry in a difficult place or a dangerous place or a less fruitful place. Or serving as a support pastor on a pastoral team rather than a lead pastor. Death is at work in you as your preferences and priorities are set aside for the sake of serving the Savior. This is what the ministry is about. Pastoral ministry is weak and dependent pastors who are dying to themselves as they serve and suffer. But check out the result. How sweet is verse 12?

"Death is at work in us, but life in you."

Spiritual life comes about through sacrificial death. Life in the form of conversion. Life in the form of growth in godliness. Life in the form of building up the church. Life in the form of the advance of the gospel. Life in the form of the transfer of the gospel to the next generation. Death at work in us, life in you.

This is how the local church is built.

If you look behind every genuinely fruitful church, you will find a dying pastor.

This is how it works. And this is the only way it works: "Death is at work in us, but life in you."

It is easy to make assumptions about why a church is influential or fruitful. It is all too easy to assume that a church is fruitful because the pastor is gifted, or because they have a great building at a great location, or because they have a team of exceptionally gifted people, or because their website is attractive, their programs well organized. It is easy to miss the truth that behind that genuinely fruitful church is a dying pastor. Not a lazy pastor, or a pastor who desires recognition, but a dying pastor.

Behind every fruitful church is a dying pastor.

D. A. Carson makes this point so well:

> [A]mong the people of God . . . it is frequently the
> leaders who are called to suffer the most. How could
> it be otherwise? We serve a crucified Messiah. . . .
> The more leaders are afflicted with weakness, suf-
> fering, perplexity, and persecution, the more it is
> evident that their vitality is nothing other than the
> life of Jesus. This has enormously positive spiri-
> tual effects on the rest of the church. The leaders'
> death means the church's life. This is why the best
> Christian leadership cannot simply be appointed.
> It is forged by God himself in the fires of suffering,
> taught in the school of tears. There are no shortcuts.[6]

There are no shortcuts. Those are the conditions of ministry. Paul understood the conditions of ministry and the purpose of God in and through those conditions. That strengthened his resolve. And in the midst of those harsh conditions of pastoral ministry, he became aware of the *but not* sustaining grace of God in his life.

3. The Hope of Christian Ministry

Finally, Paul's heart was strengthened by the hope of Christian ministry. We see this in verses 16 through 18. Paul does not lose heart because he maintains an eternal perspective. Endurance in ministry is rooted in an eternal perspective. Maintaining an eternal perspective protects pastors from losing heart.

The opposite is also true: the absence of an eternal perspective leaves you vulnerable to discouragement, disillusionment, and despair. Paul doesn't lose heart because he realizes that the proclamation of the gospel and the service and suffering in the cause of the gospel are producing something in him—he calls it "an eternal weight of glory." As Paul studied and gave careful attention to the unseen future, he became aware there was this inner work of renewal taking place that foreshadowed his future resurrection.

But as Paul contemplated the glorious future that awaited him, he also offered this poignant assessment of the present: "our outer self is wasting away." At present we are not only experiencing all kinds of weakness and suffering, we are wasting away.

All of us over fifty are becoming increasingly aware of this fact! The sad thing is Paul's wasting away probably had to do with being beaten and stoned and shipwrecked. I am just . . . wasting away. My friends are wasting away. In fact, this has become a regularly scheduled topic of our conversation. Every time we are together we give each other "wasting away" updates. "How is your back? Anyone have a new injury to report or an operation scheduled? I need a new prescription for these glasses."

But look at the difference an eternal perspective makes to those who are wasting away. Here is the hope it provides as Paul contemplates his present suffering and compares it with future glory. He concludes that there is no comparison. Yes, he is experiencing severe suffering. Yes, he is wasting away as he seeks to advance the gospel. But as he peers into the unseen future, he decides that his present suffering is "light and momentary" compared to the eternal weight of glory that is to come.

This isn't my impulse when making comparisons. When I encounter someone experiencing difficulty, I normally offer a different comparison: "Well, you know, it could be worse. I mean, I know you have it bad, but let me just tell you about somebody else I know . . ."

But Paul makes a completely different kind of comparison, a comparison that completely alters our perspective: light and momentary trouble versus eternal weight of glory. No contest! One so far outshines the other that there really is no comparison at all!

This comparison is all the more shocking if we keep in mind the nature and severity of his suffering. Keep in mind that Paul's suffering was real and it was severe. Imagine spending a few hours listening to him describe his life. You would come away from time with Paul resolved never to complain about your sufferings again. Who has a story that can top his? When this man says struck down, you see the scars on his body from rods and stones. He can tell you firsthand what it's like to be imprisoned. Shipwrecked. Starving. Sleepless. Paul's life is like some kind of brutal reality TV show except that it was, well, reality.

And yet, after providing us with an extended list of all manner and variety of suffering, he goes on to identify his trials as "light and momentary." *Say what?* This list doesn't sound "light and momentary" to me! And neither do my own trials in ministry feel "light and momentary" at the time I am experiencing them. So how can Paul say this?

Paul can only call his significant hardships "light and momentary" because he is comparing them to future glory. And in order for you and me to have this perspective, we have to *look*. We have to look in the right place. We have to look where Paul tells us he is looking in verse 18: to the glories of an unseen future, purchased by Christ's work on the cross. Paul endures the affliction of the present visible world by fixing his gaze on things unseen.

It sounds paradoxical to look at things unseen, and it is. But that is the essence of faith. It takes faith to look beyond our present sufferings, to see the eternal weight of glory, and to compare them rightly, so that we can say that our present sufferings are light and momentary.

If I do not consider my own troubles as light and momentary I am not looking in the right place. I am not focusing my gaze on the glories of the unseen future. The older you get, the more important this becomes. Because the longer you go on in pastoral ministry, the more you will suffer, the more you will find you are wasting away, and the more you will need to look to things unseen.

Contemplating this future glory transforms our perspective of the present and alters our assessment of affliction, bewilderment, persecution, and discouragement. But to lay hold of this sustaining grace we must look to the unseen, we must direct our attention to eternity future, looking to the eternal purpose of God and not preoccupied with the trials of life and ministry.

Pastor, where are you looking? The temptation for all of us is to look at our sin, our failures, our unfavorable assessment of our sermon, or our discouragement over the spiritual state of our congregation, our trials, our wasting away. The list is endless. But if you look in any of those places your circumstances will seem heavy and endless instead of light and momentary. And you will lose heart. But if

you look into the unseen, into future glory, it will have a transforming, strengthening effect on your soul. When, by the grace of God,
we *look*, we will not lose heart.

Conclusion

It won't be long until you bomb another sermon. (And unlike the
friend I told you about at the beginning of this chapter, I really do
know what it is like to bomb when I preach!) It won't be long until
you feel ineffective in counseling. Or someone leaves your church.
Or your church doesn't grow numerically. Or you encounter suffering on some scale you didn't expect. If we are not going to lose heart,
we need to be constantly infused with the wonder of our calling
to this ministry of proclaiming the gospel. We need to remember
the context of our ministry: death at work in us, life at work in our
church. And we need to fix our eyes on the hope of Christian ministry, that eternal weight of glory that far outweighs the sufferings of
today. We will find fresh hope in the knowledge that we have this
ministry by the mercy of God, and we won't lose heart.

Testimony: Sonia Jenkins

My name is Sonia Jenkins. I grew up without my biological father in a home with an alcoholic mother and multiple stepfathers. My mother and I were the entertainment at the local bar, where I began singing around the age of six. Not surprisingly, I grew into a promiscuous, drinking, and drug-using teenage girl. I was pregnant at the age of seventeen. My boyfriend and eventual husband, Toby, and I decided to keep our child, but the partying did not stop. Toby was an alcoholic who drank every night, and on weekends it was even worse.

On a Friday night in August of 1998 Toby and I had a huge party at our house where we had drinks and every type of drug. We also had our three-year-old and four-month-old sons at this party. Earlier that afternoon I had told Toby that something had to change. We could not continue to live this way.

In the midst of all this, the local evangelical pastor faithfully visited and shared the gospel with us, even walking through beer cans to get to our house. The Sunday after our party we decided to go to church. As the speaker spoke on Christians being salt of the earth and light of the world, God revealed the true condition of my heart. At the age of twenty-one, Christ came in to rule my life forever. On the way home my husband was furious. However, that afternoon as I prepared to go back to church for the evening service, he decided to go with me. Thank the Lord, he saved Toby that night! Our lives have never been the same. My boys are now seventeen and fourteen years old and both are believers. My husband, Toby Jenkins, believe it or not, is the senior pastor of First Baptist Church in Henryville, Indiana.

Although I am not proud of the person that I once was, God has used my past as a witness to reach others. His Word does not go out void. This gospel contains the power of God to change lives. Don't underestimate the gospel because God's grace is sufficient for the vilest offenders.

7

HOPE AND THE FULFILLMENT OF THE GOSPEL

Matt Chandler

Scripture quotations in this chapter are from ESV.

Hope is necessary for all who have put trust and faith in Jesus Christ, but I believe hope is especially important for those whose work is Christian ministry. Many pastors are exhausted. They are at their wits' end. They are not sure how they can make it another day. A letter of resignation is half written, and they have a file in their desk drawer with a list of people that they hope God will "take home." These men are ready to leave their calling and ministry.

I, too, pastor a church. I, too, am on the ground, bleeding right along with these other men.

But in the midst of all this, there is a refrain from God's Word that can encourage and edify the weary pastor. God says to pastors everywhere, "I am here. I have not abandoned you. I have not left you to your own devices. And I will fulfill all my promises to you."

It's this hope that a pastor needs, the hope that God will complete what he has begun in us and through us.

It is tempting to think that this hope-giving refrain is always for some *other* pastor down the street. We do not listen very well sometimes. But all the while God says to each of us, "Hey, I am talking to you, dummy. Do not be such the shepherd's shepherd that you cannot be shepherded."

The Front-Row Seat of Ministry

As pastors, we have this strange position of being able to see the glories of gospel miracles in a fallen world, like watching reconciliation occur between a man and woman who divorced ages ago, or seeing wayward sons and daughters submit their lives to Jesus Christ. We have a front-row seat to these kinds of miracles.

When we see men and women get in the water and testify, "This is what I was, and this is what Christ has done," we are seeing pictures of how these people have been taken out of the kingdom of darkness and brought into the kingdom of the beloved Son (Col. 1). The Holy Spirit of God has illuminated their hearts and minds. And we get to watch the spectacular results of that regeneration.

Simultaneously, we pastors are a kind of spiritual first responder to the tragedies and chaos of a world gone awry. There was a one-month period last Christmas when this became especially evident to me. A couple in our church had an eight-year-old autistic boy who had a bad cavity. They took him to the dentist, he had an allergic reaction to the medicine, and he died. We went to be with them, and all we could do was hug and cry and listen to their questions. There are not really answers; there are only comforting words. "He is good. I know he is good. I cannot see it all, but I know he is good."

We hardly had that family settled into care before we received another phone call. This time it was the family of a three-year-old who one year earlier had received a heart transplant. Then out of nowhere her body started rejecting the new heart. Again, we rushed over to care for them, and soon thereafter came another funeral.

The next weekend I got to church and preached. Preaching is such a refuge to me. I can feel God's power and his presence. I feel at home there. I feel synced up with him. I also feel this way in study and in evangelism, but when I get in front of a gathering, I feel an angst and a hope that makes me want to explode. So I preached, and it felt good just to be in the presence of God in that way, and to proclaim his victory, even in those difficult circumstances.

I walked off the stage, and my wife and I began talking with a beautiful young girl in our church. Her parents were divorced for seven years. Then her mom was saved and started to pursue her ex-husband for seven more years. He said to her over and over, "I am not having it, I am not having it, you cheated on me, you cheated on me." Then God saved him, and their marriage was reconciled. They brought their kids back together into a beautiful house. We talked with this girl for fifteen minutes about her growing relationship with Jesus, and how, through her modeling work, she was sharing the gospel in a domain of society that is dark. There was such victory in all of this.

Then that evening, she went out with some friends. They took a ride in a little prop plane to view Christmas lights high above Dallas. They landed. She was discombobulated, stepped out of the plane, and walked into the rotating propeller. I had gone home after preaching, where my wife and I were sitting on the couch, catching up on how we were dealing emotionally with everything. Then we received this call and quickly went up to the hospital to be with her and her parents and pray with them.

Did you catch all of that? I do the first funeral for an eight-year-old; I do a second for a three-year-old; I preach and proclaim God's glory; and then I hear about this young lady's accident. I personally have an eight-year-old and a three-year-old. Doing the funeral of small children the same ages as mine does something to me. It adds a weight that prompts a clingy-with-my-kids response. How do you maintain hope in a month like this?

I have not even mentioned the church discipline cases, the person who loves my preaching and the other person who hates my preaching, the deadlines, the elder who needs to be addressed, and everything else. The world is broken, and we pastors have a front-row seat.

Most of the time, pastors are right in after the paramedics. Sometimes we are in before them because the damage is deep but it does not require paramedics. Sometimes it is a relationship that was burned to the ground. Sometimes it is a man's sinfulness that finally found him out despite the fact that he has been sitting up front for years, hearing your appeal to repent, all the while walking secretly in sin.

The Pastor's Need for Hope

It is unbelievably important for the man of God who shepherds the people of God to have his hope anchored in the right place. This hope is not futuristic; it is here now. Early on, God told us he was going to fix this mess. Take a look at Genesis 3, Genesis 12, Genesis 17, Genesis 49, Numbers 24, Deuteronomy 17–18, 2 Samuel 7, Isaiah 7, Isaiah 9, Isaiah 53, and many others. In these chapters, there is a refrain which gets sounded over many hundreds of years that a rescue is coming, that a freedom is coming, that a transformation of hearts is coming. And then, he came. He actually showed up. God fulfills all of these promises through the life, death, and resurrection of Jesus Christ.

We need Christ's perfect life, and we need him to die our death and rise from the grave, showing that the bill is completely paid.

Then Christ comes and gets us. He came and opened up my heart. I was not looking for him. He was not on my radar. I certainly never thought I would be a preacher. I was a bit of a mocker and thought the whole Christian thing was a bit goofy. Yet he called. This is what he does. I continue to marvel at Romans 8:30 where it says, "And those whom he predestined he also called."

To tell the story briefly, the US government decided that the Chandler family, a military family, needed to move from California's Bay Area to Galveston, Texas. So we moved. Once in school, I just happened to be assigned a football locker next to a guy named Jeff Faircloth who boldly shared the gospel with me. He was ferocious. He had no fear in the world. "I need to tell you about Jesus. When do you want to do it?" He was going to share the gospel with me, but he gave me the freedom of deciding when that would happen. I then got involved at First Baptist Church of Texas City, where God continued to woo and call me.

Here's what's crazy, though. I did not know God was wooing and calling. I was that weird character who is probably present in many churches, who keeps criticizing, but who also keeps coming. I would leave church with Jeff and tell him how bad, ignorant, and dumb it was, only to say "yes" when he offered to pick me up. I would tell him, "I just think you guys are morons. I can't believe you actually buy that stuff. Next Wednesday at six o'clock? Yeah sure. Pick me up." This is how God calls and woos. This is how he rescues sinners.

Do you see our cause for hope? God did all that. I did not seek out Jeff. I did not seek out a church home. I did not want to get to the bottom of this God thing. He just invaded. He did not ask for my approval or opinion. In fact, he did not even answer all my questions before he owned me. I might have been saying, "Well, what about . . ." to which God replied, "What about nothing!" And BAM, he showed me himself, and I agreed with him.

In those seasons where I feel like hope is being sucked out of me, I try to remember that he came and got me. This was not my idea. It was not my covenant. I did not ask my way into this thing. He rescued me. He pulled me up from the muck and the mire. And he did not do all of that in order to destroy me.

My tendency is to downshift into thinking like the nation of Israel did in the wilderness. "You brought me out into the desert and then you left me." I wonder how many pastors feel abandoned like that.

When I feel hope slipping, I have to remind myself that he brought me to this place, and the Spirit does not lead where the Spirit does not empower. If I am weary, it is usually because I have tried to own something that God has not asked me to own, and I have put my hope in myself instead of him.

But our hope must rest in his saving power, his calling, his election, his empowerment, his wooing, and his delight to rescue. Not only that, our hope should be in the fact that he fulfills his promises and his purposes, and that brings us to Revelation 21.

The Hope of Fulfillment

Graeme Goldsworthy said, "Hope without a time of fulfillment is a delusion."[1] Christians are not a delusional people. We are not gambling by putting our hope in the gospel. We are not just hoping that this thing called Christianity works out. We know that the fulfillment of all things is coming. We have already seen God make promises and deliver on his promises. We see that throughout the Scriptures, and that is what we are promised in Revelation 21.

> Then I saw a new heaven and a new earth, for the
> first heaven and the first earth had passed away, and
> the sea was no more. And I saw the holy city, new

Jerusalem, coming down out of heaven from God, prepared as a bride adorned for her husband. And I heard a loud voice from the throne saying, "Behold, the dwelling place of God is with man. He will dwell with them, and they will be his people, and God himself will be with them as their God. He will wipe away every tear from their eyes, and death shall be no more, neither shall there be mourning, nor crying, nor pain anymore, for the former things have passed away."

And he who was seated on the throne said, "Behold, I am making all things new." Also he said, "Write this down, for these words are trustworthy and true." And he said to me, "It is done! I am the Alpha and the Omega, the beginning and the end. To the thirsty I will give from the spring of the water of life without payment. The one who conquers will have this heritage, and I will be his God and he will be my son. But as for the cowardly, the faithless, the detestable, as for murderers, the sexually immoral, sorcerers, idolaters, and all liars, their portion will be in the lake that burns with fire and sulfur, which is the second death." (vv. 1–8)

This picture of the new heaven and earth is beautiful. It's not that the old heaven and earth get blown up like the Death Star in *Star Wars*. Rather, the heaven and earth are renewed. The point is, this is not ethereal. This is not *Tom & Jerry*. It is not us wearing robes and playing harps on a cloud. It is something of the world we know being made new.

Furthermore, this beautiful picture fulfills a number of God's Old Testament promises. Isaiah 35:1 tells us that the desert shall blossom like the crocus. Have you ever flown over the Sahara

Desert? I have en route to Sudan for our church's missions work. It amazes me how long you will look at nothing but sand. Ultimately, the desert is representative of death. The only life that does exist in a desert is so spectacular we put it on the Discovery Channel, like the one little lizard that survives by eating sand. But when God's work is done and the day of fulfillment comes, the Sahara is going to bloom and smell like the crocus.

Amos 9:13 says that the plowman shall overtake the reaper, and the mountains shall drop sweet wine. Several times a year, I have to fly to Seattle, and we always fly right next to Mount Rainier. Being from Dallas, it always makes me shudder. There are no mountains in Dallas; we barely have hills. Flying past this majestic and spectacular thing poking through the clouds creates awe in me. But when God's work is done and the day of fulfillment comes, sweet wine will come from those craggy rocks and snow.

Isaiah 65 promises that, one day, there will be no more sounds of weeping on the earth (v. 19), that the days of God's people shall be like the days of a tree (v. 22), and that the wolf and lamb shall feed together (v. 25). Do you know why that last promise is significant? The wolf feeds with the lamb now, but it's not the same thing. On that day the wolf will feed with the lamb in a very different way than he is now. The violence that is so woven into the world that we know will be lifted and gone. Isaiah next says that the great lion will chew straw like the oxen (v. 25). The violence of the universe will settle into sweet peace.

Isaiah 11:9 and 65:25 promise that no one will hurt or destroy anything on God's holy mountain.

Habakkuk 2:14 says that the earth will be filled with a knowledge of the Lord as the waters cover the sea. I don't know the last time you were out on the sea, but there is water everywhere.

Then, turning to the promises of the New Testament, I love 1 Corinthians 15. The Lord used this text to minister to me during the eighteen months that I was pounded with chemotherapy treatment for cancer. First Corinthians 15 promises us resurrected bodies, imperishable ones. It is important for you to understand that your abs are going to betray you. Work out all you want; eat all the spinach you want; do all the crunches you want. Your body is going to betray you. If you live long enough, Ecclesiastes 12 says, you will start to hate that you woke up because the world will terrify you. But the gospel promises us imperishable bodies.

What hope do weary pastors have? We have the hope that one day all the promises of the gospel will be fulfilled.

The Hope of Seeing Christ

There will be a day when we no longer look forward to this grand day, because we will be there. Doesn't it sound amazing? How spectacular will that day be!

If you go back through your Bible, and look at the texts where a person hungers for God, desires for God, seeks after God, you will find a person in pain. The opening verse in Psalm 42, "As a deer pants for flowing streams, so pants my soul for you, O God," is not a cute text. The psalmist's soul is cast down. The same is true of Psalm 27:4: "One thing have I asked of the LORD, that will I seek after: that I may dwell in the house of the LORD all the days of my life, to gaze upon the beauty of the LORD." These words do not belong on a coffee cup. That guy is in agony.

Or think of Paul who says he longs to know Christ in Philippians 3. He hungers to know Jesus and to see his face, and he works hard to pursue him. But on that day, his hunger and pursuit will be over because Jesus will be right there.

We will not have to fight, scrap, and press down our flesh to choke out that sin in us. Jesus will be right there. We will possess a holiness that is hard to get our minds around now, so poisoned are we by the perversions of our day and age. That is a spectacular thought.

My wife and I have been reading *The Chronicles of Narnia* by C. S. Lewis with our children. In fact, my son just clued into what's going on: "Wait! Aslan is Jesus!" I love the last paragraph of *The Last Battle*. Lewis writes,

> The things that began to happen after that were so great and beautiful that I cannot write them. And for us this is the end of all the stories, and we can most truly say that they all lived happily ever after. But for them it was only the beginning of the real story. All their life in this world and all their adventures in Narnia had only been the cover and the title page: now at last they were beginning Chapter One of the Great Story, which no one on earth has read: which goes on for ever: in which every chapter is better than the one before.[2]

When I began to get my head and heart around all this, what God has already delivered me from, how he called and wooed me, where I am now, what God has promised us, and what we will find at the finish line, then I get restful. I think, *Yes, I am going to get to rest. There is not going to be this kind of toil, death, or conflict.* All those stories of death and pain that I shared earlier will be gone. I will not have a front-row seat to carnage any longer. I will have a front-row seat only to glory.

What hope do weary pastors have? We have the hope of seeing Christ and becoming like him.

The Hope of Beholding the Bride

But God does not stop there. He shows us something else. Not only do we have Jesus Christ right there; not only do we have the glory of God right there; not only is there no more death, no more mourning, and no more tears; but then an angel comes in and says, "Come, I will show you the Bride, the wife of the Lamb" (Rev. 21:9).

Why is that significant? Think about where we began. A lot of us pastors are bleeding pretty badly on the bride right now, are we not? We have been called by God to wash her in the water of the Word, to defend her, to protect her, to put watchmen on the wall, and to fight for her maturity. I do not how it's going for other pastors, but depending on the day, I can feel like God is moving profoundly or I can feel like David when he wonders, "Where are you, Lord? How long will you forsake us?"

But in Revelation 21 we learn that we will behold the bride made beautiful. After all this work, all this effort, all this delight-fueled discipline, all this engagement, all the courage that it takes to sit someone down and confront them lovingly about their sin, we will get to see the fruit of God's work through Christ in the Holy Spirit as executed by you and me.

At some level, this will be more spectacular than seeing the doors swing open and beholding your human bride. I say this knowing that my wife will read this. Surely, that was a spectacular day. But this is the day where so much of your hope, so many of your longings, so much of the fire that has burned in you so that you have been willing to be paid next to nothing and to work hard long hours dealing with deeply spiritual, seemingly intractable issues, are finally fulfilled. God has birthed in those of us who are pastors a passion for his bride, and on that day we get to see her made perfect.

Consider what we will see:

And he carried me away in the Spirit to a great, high
mountain, and showed me the holy city Jerusalem
coming down out of heaven from God, having the
glory of God, its radiance like a most rare jewel, like
a jasper, clear as crystal. It had a great, high wall,
with twelve gates, and at the gates twelve angels,
and on the gates the names of the twelve tribes of
the sons of Israel were inscribed—on the east three
gates, on the north three gates, on the south three
gates, and on the west three gates. And the wall of
the city had twelve foundations, and on them were
the twelve names of the twelve apostles of the Lamb.

And the one who spoke with me had a measur-
ing rod of gold to measure the city and its gates and
walls. The city lies foursquare, its length the same
as its width. And he measured the city with his
rod, 12,000 stadia. Its length and width and height
are equal. He also measured its wall, 144 cubits
by human measurement, which is also an angel's
measurement. The wall was built of jasper, while
the city was pure gold, like clear glass. The foundations of the wall of the city were adorned with every
kind of jewel. The first was jasper, the second sap-
phire, the third agate, the fourth emerald, the fifth
onyx, the sixth carnelian, the seventh chrysolite, the
eighth beryl, the ninth topaz, the tenth chrysoprase,
the eleventh jacinth, the twelfth amethyst. And the
twelve gates were twelve pearls, each of the gates
made of a single pearl, and the street of the city was
pure gold, like transparent glass. (Rev. 21:10–21)

Before jumping into this passage, it's worth thinking back to the
first time we see the church in the book of Revelation—chapters
2 and 3. Those chapters give us a picture of a church that lines up

with what we see in our ministries now. In Ephesus, they had great doctrine but forgot their first love, which is terrifying to me. Sadly, it is not uncommon. Sound doctrine without a love for Jesus Christ ceases to be sound doctrine. I don't know how you begin loving a truth about a man and not love the man of whom that truth is about. It is devastating to the soul and to the bride.

In Smyrna, they faced tribulation and poverty.

In Pergamum, they held to teaching that went against the grain and hope of the gospel.

In Thyatira, they loved the sensuality of Jezebel and sexual immorality.

In Sardis, they were dead. They were unmoved by the majesty of God.

In Philadelphia, they had little power, but they clung tightly to Jesus Christ.

In Laodicea, probably the most famous one, they were lukewarm and indifferent toward the things of God. They considered themselves rich and prosperous, but Jesus says they were pitiful, poor, blind, and naked.

Some scholars say that these are ages of the church, or the seasons of the church. But I read these chapters and think, "That one is Tuesday. I saw it in home group. That one is Wednesday . . ." You know this when you do ministry on the ground. There are people who sit in our services week in and week out, hear the gospel proclaimed, and are dead to it, unmoved by it, want nothing of it. There are other people who have given into the sensuality of this age, and even though you rebuke them and point them toward holiness, they do not hear. On and on we could go through each church and what I can see in my own church. These are the churches in Revelation 2 and 3.

But that is not what we just read in Revelation 21, is it? The first time I read this text, I kept wondering, *Okay, so here's the church, but where is everyone? There are all these jewels and pearls and foundations, but did nobody make the cut?* Then I remembered Paul in 1 Corinthians 3:

> For no one can lay a foundation other than that
> which is laid, which is Jesus Christ. Now if anyone
> builds on the foundation with gold, silver, pre-
> cious stones, wood, hay, straw—each one's work
> will become manifest, for the Day will disclose it,
> because it will be revealed by fire, and the fire will
> test what sort of work each one has done. (vv. 11–13)

I sometimes find myself identifying people in these terms: "That is a gold guy right there. There's an emerald." Most of the time, I feel like I am trying to put wood and straw together with some glue and sprinkles. I can get into a pattern in ministry where, though I see some of God's victories, I look at the whole and think I only see straw, wood, and stubble; so much that will be burned. But when time passes I begin to see what God is really doing, and how I can trust that he is accomplishing something good through the steady and faithful work of cleansing, shaping, and purifying of his bride.

I look at this text and find my heart rejoices in the fact that the crown jewel of the new creation is the bride of Christ. There will be a day that she ceases to be a suffering church and becomes the church triumphant. Today, we are one day closer. We were faithful yesterday, and now we are one day closer. We take it one day at a time, with new mercies every morning until all things are fulfilled.

What hope do weary pastors have? We have the hope of behold-ing the bride made perfect.

The Hope of Unmediated Worship

John's vision does not stop. Look at what comes next in this text.

> And I saw no temple in the city, for its temple is the
> Lord God the Almighty and the Lamb. And the city
> has no need of sun or moon to shine on it, for the
> glory of God gives it light, and its lamp is the Lamb.
> (Rev. 21:22–23)

As a pastor who preaches the Bible, I am, in a sense, dealing with shadows. "God is like this. This is what he does. This is what his Bible says." In Revelation 21 there is no working with shadows. There he is. We will hear him directly, and we will worship him directly. We will not need a tabernacle. We will not need a temple. We will not have to come together at 10 o'clock to worship him. No, he is there, and we are gathered with him. There will not be a certain time that worship will take place, or a time in which we will especially enjoy the ever-increasing joy of the presence of God because we will always enjoy him. The joy of his presence will always increase. It will always grow.

I have been in rooms of Christians where we were really "getting after" the Lord where we were worshiping and it was evident that his Spirit was among us. But even in those moments, as I screamed at the top of my lungs in my non-singing voice, I could feel myself hit a ceiling. I could feel my body get tired and my voice wear out. It was as if I had this thing in me that wanted to explode, but I could not explode.

What I understand from this text is that I get to explode. The ceiling is removed. The time constraint is removed. The physical weariness is removed, and I get to chase after him always. That is a spectacular picture.

What hope do weary pastors have? We have the hope of unmediated worship.

The Hope of Restoration and Unity

Our chapter gives us still more reason to hope. We keep reading:

> By its light will the nations walk, and the kings of the earth will bring their glory into it, and its gates will never be shut by day—and there will be no night there. They will bring into it the glory and the honor of the nations. But nothing unclean will ever enter it, nor anyone who does what is detestable or false, but only those who are written in the Lamb's book of life. (Rev. 21:24–27)

All the pieces come together here. "By [this] light will the nations walk." Think about how hard finding unity amidst diversity can be, whether in our society or even in churches. Think about how hard it is to get past cultural hurdles. Think about how much strategy goes into overcoming those things. On this day, all the nations will walk by the light of the Lamb. Think about all the glories of the nations. On this day, all that is beautiful and right in this world will be restored, renewed, made right, and put in its place.

I can marvel at this as I travel. My wife, Lauren, and I spent twelve days in southern Sudan a couple of years ago. Sudan has been ripped to shreds by a nasty civil war over the last few decades. It is a country that has the glorious ambition to *become* a third-world country. It is larger than Texas and has three miles of paved road. It is not safe, and war is never far from peoples' memory or from reality. I remember thinking, *This is all so broken.* The complexities of fixing it baffle the wisest minds. War has killed millions, displaced many more, and a country once lush and vibrant has been turned to dust. Is this not hopeless?

In fact, Revelation 21 promises a restoration of harmony that now seems impossible. How much better, more beautiful, more spectacular will all things be when the glory of men and nations are restored and put together!

What hope do weary pastors have? We have the hope that all things will be restored and the glorious diversity of humankind will be united with the Father, Son, and Spirit.

Stop Hedging Your Bets

I want to get my mind on this coming day more often, not as a type of escapism, but in a way that drives me to work and rest today. When I read this passage, I don't think, *I just want to die and get there.* Instead I think, *I want to be faithful and get there.* I don't want to get there unless God wants me to get there right now. If he does, then let's go! I have said for a long time, if my time is up, why would I want to be here? "What about your children?" I have been asked. If my time is up, they do not need me. They need what's next. I am not saying that tritely. I would love to be an old man. You can get away with stuff when you are older that you cannot get away with when you are younger. I want the freedom to say something crazy and have people respond, "You know, he's just old." I want to walk my daughters down the aisle. I want grandchildren. How sweet of a gig is grandparenting! You don't have to discipline and shape them. You get to sprinkle candy on them and send them back home. I want all of this. If my time is up, I want to go. But if my time is not up, I want to be faithful. We pastors have the charge placed on us to guard the purity of the bride. So the promise of Revelation does not make me want to escape; it makes me want to be faithful to protect her purity until we get there.

Often our hope drains because we are not looking high enough at what God is doing or accomplishing. Instead, we can hedge our bets, and I believe that many pastors are. You *kind of* believe this day is coming, but you do not fully believe it. You want to get one foot into this Revelation 21 world, and you want to get all the good stuff here too—just in case. You straddle these two worlds.

That is a miserable way to do life. My encouragement is to sell out. Put your hope fully in this picture of heaven.

The apostle Paul had this view of heaven. That is why he could call trouble here "light and momentary." Think about that: light and momentary? Really? His trials were brutal. Have you ever wondered what it would be like to be shipwrecked, and then climb onto an island, and then get bitten by a snake? If there has ever been a guy who gets to say, "Come on, pastors!" it is Paul on the island. Yet he called his troubles light and momentary. Paul didn't straddle the fence. He did not hedge his bets. He said, "I am all in. If the resurrection is not true, we are to be pitied because we are all in."

How do we stop hedging our bets and throw ourselves all in? We rest in this vision. We think on it and believe in it. We believe this is going to happen. It is not ethereal. As assuredly as last week became this week, this day is going to happen. We will get there. We will see this city.

Hope is important for the man of God. Hope is important for those who shepherd the bride of Christ.

Find hope in that God keeps his promises. Find hope in that Jesus Christ came and that he saved you. Find hope in that you have been empowered by the Holy Spirit one day at a time. Find hope in the fact that there is a finish line. There is a day when all things will be made new. The former things, the dark things, the bloody things, the hard things will be remembered no more (Isa. 65).

I look forward to seeing you there—on this side or the other. It bothers some people, particularly my wife, when I say, "I will see you later—on this side or the other." I do want to see you here now, but even more let us marvel at what God has prepared for us then.

We are buffoons, yet God has entrusted us with all this?! Praise him.

Testimony: George Paz

My name is George Paz. My biological father was a "coyote," that is, someone who smuggles drugs and people across the US–Mexico border. My mother and I snuck into the United States when I was two. We lived in a cold garage on the money she made as a hotel housekeeper. We were illegal until she married a US citizen when I was nine.

For the next three years I heard her get beat every night by my stepfather. I finally met my biological father at the age of fourteen a month before he died of alcohol. Years of anger, violence, alcohol, and drugs followed.

Several years ago I picked up a copy of the book *Left Behind* at a thrift store. I didn't find the gospel in that book, but it made me curious enough to visit a nearby church. In the middle of the second sermon I heard, I realized that I deserved God's wrath for all the heinous things I had done and the people I had hurt. Only God's grace had allowed me to live up to this point so that I would be forgiven. Not everyone remembers the moment they were converted, but I do. It was a moment in which a great weight was lifted off my shoulders, and I felt an inexpressible joy. After the sermon, the last song was "Nothing but the Blood of Jesus." I fell to the floor sobbing before Almighty God.

After my conversion, I began to wage war against my old sin. I also shared the gospel with my mother who became a Christian a year and a half ago. Today, I serve in the US Navy, and I pray the Lord gives me the opportunity to become a pastor and preach the gospel until the day I die.

We can debate the complexities of immigration another day. But never underestimate the power of the gospel, even in the life of an illegal immigrant.

8

GLORY, MAJESTY, DOMINION, AND AUTHORITY KEEP US SAFE FOR EVERLASTING JOY

John Piper

Scripture quotations in this chapter are from ESV.

This chapter has two parts. In the first part, I will try to draw you into my amazement that I am still a Christian and still love the ministry of the Word. And perhaps you will feel the same about yourself. In the second part, I will try to draw you into an analysis of how that happened. My text is the book of Jude, and the focus will fall mainly on verses 24 and 25.

> Now to him who is able to keep you from stumbling
> and to present you blameless before the presence of
> his glory with great joy, to the only God, our Savior,
> through Jesus Christ our Lord, be glory, majesty,
> dominion, and authority, before all time and now
> and forever. Amen.

How God Has Kept Me

First, let me try to draw you into my amazement that I am still a
Christian and still love the ministry of God's Word and the spiritual
calling I have as a husband and father. This year I complete sixty
years as a believer, thirty-two years pastoring Bethlehem Baptist
Church, forty-four years of marriage to Noël, and forty years of
being a father. These are momentous days for me as we plan for
my successor to assume responsibilities at Bethlehem. If there is a
Together for the Gospel in 2014, and if I am invited to come, I will
not be speaking as the preaching pastor of Bethlehem.

When I think about finishing these laps in my race, I am simply
amazed that I have lasted. Lasted as Christian, lasted as a pastor,
lasted as a husband and father. For you to begin to grasp why I feel
this way, it may help to read an excerpt from my journal from 1986.
What you are going to read offers a picture of the sort of emotional
vulnerability that I have dealt with all my life. There have been seasons when it seemed like I could not last.

When I wrote this I was forty years old and had been at the
church for six years. I had been married eighteen years. I had four
sons, ages fourteen, eleven, seven, and three.

> Am I under attack by Satan to abandon my post at
> Bethlehem? Or is this the stirring of God to cause
> me to consider another ministry? Or is this God's
> way of answering so many prayers recently that we
> must go a different way at BBC than building? I
> simply loathe the thought of leading the church
> through a building program. For two years I have
> met for hundreds of hours on committees. I have
> never written a poem about it. It is deadening to my
> soul. I am a thinker. A writer. A preacher. A poet and

songwriter. At least these are the avenues of love and service where my heart flourishes. . . .

Can I be the pastor of a church moving through a building program? Yes, by dint of massive will-power and some clear indications from God that this is the path of greatest joy in him long term. But now I feel very much without those indications. The last two years [the long-range planning committee was started in August 1984] have left me feeling very empty.

The church is looking for a vision for the future—and I do not have it. The one vision that the staff zeroed in on during our retreat Monday and Tuesday of this week (namely, building a sanctuary) is so unattractive to me today that I do not see how I could provide the leadership and inspiration for it.

Does this mean that my time at BBC is over? Does it mean that there is a radical alternative unforeseen? Does it mean that I am simply in the pits today and unable to feel the beauty and power and joy and fruitfulness of an expanded facility and ministry?

O Lord, have mercy on me. I am so discouraged. I am so blank. I feel like there are opponents on every hand, even when I know that most of my people are for me. I am so blind to the future of the church. O Father, am I blind because it is not my future? Perhaps I shall not even live out the year, and you are sparing the church the added burden of a future I had made and could not complete?

I do not doubt for a moment your goodness or power or omnipotence in my life or in the life of the church. I confess that the problem is mine. The weakness is in me. The blindness is in my eyes. The sin—O reveal to me my hidden faults!—is mine and mine the blame. Have mercy, Father. Have mercy on me. I must preach on Sunday, and I can scarcely lift my head.

That was twenty-six years ago. There have been worse days. Days when the marriage was under attack. Days when the soul was so numb I feared for my faith. So, looking back, I am amazed that I have lasted.

If my faith in Jesus, and my eagerness to know him and his Word, and my thrill at preaching, and my love for the church, and my fitness for ministry and for heaven, and my sexual continence, and my spiritual marriage commitment to Noël depended decisively on me, I would have ceased to be a Christian long ago. I would have ceased to care about the Word of God or thrill at exposition. I would have given up on the church and ceased to be fit for ministry or heaven. I would have given myself to sexual indulgence and ceased to be married to Noël.

I have no doubt about this. If the decisive cause of my faithfulness to Christ in any of those expressions must come from me, it will not come, because it is not there. Therefore, I am amazed that I am still a Christian and love the ministry. And I feel some sense of the wonder that Jude seems to feel:

> Now to him who has been mighty to keep me from stumbling and to present me blameless before the presence of his glory with great joy, to the only God, my Savior, through Jesus Christ my Lord, be glory, majesty, dominion, and authority, before all time and now and forever. Amen. (vv. 24–25)

That is what it took to keep me a Christian for sixty years, and to keep me alive in the pastoral ministry at Bethlehem for thirty-two years, and to keep me obediently married for forty-four years—glory and majesty and dominion and authority, working before the creation ever existed, and working every present moment of my life, and working into the future to keep me holy and happy for ever.

That's what it took to keep me from falling—and what it will take to get me home before the presence of his glory, blameless and full of unbridled joy. And that's what it will take to keep you believing, and ministering, and holy to the end of your days, and then get you home.

This is the way doxologies work. They refer first to something that God has done or will do, and then they ascribe attributes to God that account for that action, or are expressed in the action. So, for example, you might say, "Now to him who fashioned the intricacies of the human eye and every molecule and atom in it—to him belong infinite, inscrutable wisdom and skill." Or you might say, "Now to him who adopts dirty, abandoned, rebellious children into his family—to him belong compassion and boundless mercy."

In other words, the attributes that you ascribe to God are the ones that account for the action you are praising, or that come to expression in the action you are praising. His wisdom and skill are expressed in making the eye. His compassion and mercy are expressed in adopting of unworthy foundlings. These attributes account for the actions you are celebrating.

So it is in Jude 1:24–25.

> Now to him who is able to keep you from stumbling
> and to present you blameless before the presence of
> his glory with great joy, to the only God, our Savior,
> through Jesus Christ our Lord, be glory, majesty,
> dominion, and authority, before all time and now
> and forever. Amen.

Jude is celebrating three things: God keeps us from stumbling; he presents us before the glory of God blameless; and he presents us before the glory of God with great happiness. And then he says: What came to expression in these three acts of God was God's glory and majesty and power and authority. That's what it took to keep me a Christian for sixty years, and to keep me alive in the pastorate for thirty-two years. This perseverance was the effect of God's glory and majesty and power and authority.

Let's press the amazement a little further. Do we have any idea of the degree (the measure) of divine glory and majesty and power and authority that it took to give us spiritual life when we were dead (Eph. 2:5), and to keep us spiritually alive moment by moment, and to stir up that spiritual life in such ways that it resisted sins and loved holiness and pursued spiritual fruit in the life of the church?

Do we know the degree of glory and majesty and power and authority that took? No. We don't. We have no terms of measurement for such glory and majesty and power and authority. How do you quantify a Spirit creating and sustaining spirit? Or a Spirit acting on spirit to sustain the life of that spirit? Pounds of pressure? Kilowatts of electrical force? Roentgens of radiation?

God creates spiritual life when we are dead. "That which is born of the Spirit is spirit" (John 3:6). We had no spiritual life. Then the Spirit acted in us. And now we are spiritually alive. We are spirit. This is not spirit like the demons are spirit. This is Holy Spirit. This is eternal, spiritual, God-created, and God-sustained spiritual life.

And this spiritual life that we have is not ours intrinsically. It is not ours autonomously. We have this life to the degree that we have the Holy Spirit in us, and to the degree that we are united to Christ—which are interwoven realities. It is not the kind of spiritual life that we would have if the Spirit left us or we were not united to Christ. We would not be alive if we were not united to Christ by the Spirit. Our life is Christ's life. The Spirit's life.

The giving of this life, and the moment-by-moment sustaining and keeping of this life, and the stirring up of this life so that it treasures holiness and ministry is a work of God. This is why I said at the beginning, if the decisive cause of my faithfulness to Christ must come from me, it will not come, because it is not there.

I bring nothing decisive to my creation. And I bring nothing decisive to the ongoing existence of this divine spiritual life in me. I exist as a Christian by it. I did not create it. I don't keep it in being. Not any more than the universe came into existence by its own power or is upheld by its own power (Heb. 1:3).

Jude is clearly amazed at what it takes to sustain spiritual life—to keep it from collapsing and to bring it to glory blameless and happy. He must sense that what it takes to keep us believing—to keep us alive—is very great. So how do we join him in this God-exalting amazement?

How do we then measure what it took for God to bring my spiritual life into being and keep me alive and holy and happy to the day of Christ? There are only two ways that I can see that we can measure what it takes to accomplish the preservation of our spiritual life?

One is to think about the fact that creating and sustaining spiritual life is something we cannot do at all, and that God alone does it. And the difference between nothing and anything is infinite. Let me put it this way: If God says to you: Create a being with divine spiritual life and sustain it, you will say, "I can't." And you will be right. You absolutely can't. Then he does it with a word or a thought.

The difference between your absolute inability—your nothing—and his absolute ability—his something—is immeasurable. Indeed it is immeasurably great. That's the first way we can measure what it took to give us life and preserve it blameless and joyful to the day of Christ. We know we can't do it and he can. The measurement of what it took to create us and keep us alive is the distance between us and God. It is an infinite wonder that God creates and sustains our spiritual life—that I am still a Christian.

The second way we know the measurement of what it took for God to sustain our spiritual life blameless and joyful before the glory of God is that he reveals it to us in verse 25: it took glory and majesty and power and authority. If the first computation of the infinite difference between your contribution and God's contribution to your spiritual life does not make sense, then just take God's word for it. Your creation and your preservation take divine glory and majesty and power and authority. And any amount of divine glory and majesty and power and authority is infinitely greater than what you bring to your creation and preservation.

It is simply amazing that I am still a Christian and love God's Word, God's people, and my spiritual calling as husband and father.

How God Keeps Us

That's the end of part one—my effort to draw you into my amazement that I am still a Christian. Now I would like to try to draw you in to my analysis of how this happened. How does God keep us . . .

- when Paul's strategies of not losing heart (2 Cor. 4) seem remote,
- and when the language to articulate the gospel with words one more time won't come,
- and when you're depressed not just because your church has false converts, but you fear you may be one,
- and when you can remember countless times when you gave no evidence of trusting the power of the gospel to convert a neighbor, let alone a terrorist,
- and when Spirit-empowered, gospel-driven, faith-fueled effort seems as likely as flying by flapping your arms,

- and when the fuel tank of death-defying devotion to world missions seems empty,
- and when your treasure is held out to you and God says, "You can't have it,"
- and when the crown jewel of the new Jerusalem that you are trying to lead is cut in slivers by an airplane propeller, or by the seduction of the prophetess Jezebel.

How does God keep us? Keep us alive, keep us believing, keep us serving?

Notice that Jude's letter begins and ends with the assurance that God is decisively our keeper. We have already seen the end, verse 24: "Now to him who is able [who is strong] to keep you . . ." Now look at the beginning, verse 1: "Jude, a servant of Jesus Christ and brother of James, To those who are *called, beloved* in God the Father and *kept* for Jesus Christ" (emphasis added). We are *called*. We are *loved*. And we are *kept*. The *love* of God moves him to *call* his elect to himself out of death and unbelief. And those whom he calls he *keeps*.

This is exactly what Paul teaches: God keeps those whom he calls. None is lost. "[He] will sustain you to the end, guiltless in the day of our Lord Jesus Christ. God is faithful, by whom you were *called*" (1 Cor. 1:8–9, emphasis added). The called are sustained guiltless in the last day. The keeping is implicit in the call. That is what Jude means in verse 24. Then Paul says it again in Romans 8:30: "Those whom he predestined he also *called*, and those whom he called he also justified, and those whom he justified he also glorified." None of the called is lost. The called are kept. That is a rock-solid teaching of Paul and Jude.

So Jude establishes first and last the decisive work of God in keeping his own. And in between he warns against the false teachers who "pervert the grace of our God into sensuality" (v. 4), and who presume that they are saved but are destroyed because they don't "believe" (v. 5). So these professing Christians are not called and they are not kept. And the evidence that they are not called and not kept is that they don't crave Christ, they crave physical sensations. They don't prize the God of grace; they prostitute the grace of God.

Then after those many warnings, Jude tells us what we must do for ourselves (vv. 20–21) and for those we love (vv. 22–23), in order to go on being kept by God. I'm only going to deal with what we do for ourselves because this brings out the paradox of the Christian life most clearly. Verses 20–21:

> But you, beloved, building yourselves up in your
> most holy faith and praying in the Holy Spirit, keep
> yourselves in the love of God, waiting for the mercy
> of our Lord Jesus Christ that leads to eternal life.

So now, Kevin DeYoung's chapter comes into focus again. "I worked harder than any of them, though it was not I, but the grace of God that is with me" (1 Cor. 15:10). Or as Paul says in Philippians 2:12–13, "Work out your own salvation with fear and trembling, for it is God who works in you, both to will and to work for his good pleasure."

Here in Jude it goes like this: "Keep yourselves in the love of God" (v. 21), for God is the one who keeps you in his love. The order and logic are supremely important. Verse 21: the love of God called you; the love of God will keep you. Therefore, keep yourselves in the love of God. Keep yourselves in God's prior commitment to keep you.

And what does that mean? "Keep" is the main verb—the only imperative verb in verses 20–21—and the other three verbs are supporting participles, defining how Jude understands keeping ourselves in the love of God: (1) "building yourselves up in your most holy faith"; (2) "praying in the Holy Spirit"; and (3) "waiting for the mercy of our Lord Jesus Christ that leads to eternal life" (vv. 20–21).

The key words in those phrases are *faith*, *prayer*, and *waiting*. So, keep yourselves in the love of God—keep yourselves in the omnipotent commitment of God's love to keep you, by *trusting* that omnipotent commitment, by *praying* for its daily application to the specifics of your life, and by *waiting* patiently for God to finish his merciful work. You pray for God to keep you ("Preserve me, O God!"). You trust the promise that he will ("for in you I take refuge"). And you wait for his mercy.

And in none of this do you rob him of the glory and majesty and power and authority by which he decisively, faithfully, omnipotently keeps you. Because even your praying is his doing—it is by the Spirit that you pray (v. 20). And your faith is his doing, not your own, "it is the gift of God" (Eph. 2:8). Your praying for his keeping, and your trusting in his keeping, *is* his keeping.

The glory and the majesty of his keeping consists very much in the power and the authority that he has to keep you through the means of your keeping yourself in the love of God. You are not a robot. And you are not autonomous. You are a new creation, a new race. Your coming into being and your being sustained is unlike anything the world can ever experience. It is a mystery. A daily miracle. We are those who by prayer and trust keep ourselves in the commitment of God's love to keep us praying and trusting.

Which leads to one last crucial observation. God's act to keep you praying and trusting so that you remain in his love and are kept blameless and joyful for the glory of God—that act is the fulfillment of the New Covenant. "I will make with them an everlasting covenant, that I will not turn away from doing good to them. And I will put the fear of me in their hearts, that they may not turn from me" (Jer. 32:40). The New Covenant promise is that God will act so decisively for his newborn elect that they will not turn from him. They will be kept. They will pray and they will trust and they will keep themselves in the love of God. He will see to it. Our praying and trusting him to keep us is his keeping us. This is God's New Covenant promise.

And this New Covenant fulfillment in our lives was secured, purchased by the blood of Jesus Christ. "This cup is the new covenant in my blood" (1 Cor. 11:25). When Jesus died for us, all the promises of God became Yes in him (2 Cor. 1:20). He will see to it that his own will not turn from him into destruction (Jer. 32:40). He will keep them from falling. That is a blood-bought, New Covenant promise.

And that is the ultimate reason why Jude 25 says, "To the only God, our Savior, *through Jesus Christ our Lord*, be glory, majesty, dominion, and authority" (emphasis added). The glory and majesty and power and authority that it takes to keep you and me alive in Christ—to keep us praying and trusting, to keep us in the love of God—was secured for us sinners when Christ died for us. Therefore the glory and majesty and dominion and authority that keeps us from falling and presents us blameless and joyful to God is through the blood of Jesus Christ—the blood of the covenant. And therefore when we ascribe glory and majesty and dominion and authority to God, we do it through Jesus Christ.

So do not underestimate the power of the blood of Christ to keep you from falling. Its power was at work "before the foundation of the world" (Rev. 13:8), it is at work "now," and it will be at work "forever." Your keeping began before creation, it is happening now, and it will never end.

> He will not let your foot be moved; he who keeps
> you will not slumber. Behold, he who keeps Israel
> will neither slumber nor sleep.
> The Lord is your keeper; the Lord is your shade
> on your right hand. The sun shall not strike you by
> day, nor the moon by night.

> The LORD will keep you from all evil; he will
> keep your life. The LORD will keep your going out
> and your coming in from this time forth and *forever-*
> *more.* (Ps. 121:3–8, emphasis added)

He sealed that promise with the blood of his Son. Therefore, keep yourself in the love of God.

Testimony: John Folmar

My name is John Folmar. I grew up in a church-going home in North Carolina. But the churches we attended were not clear on the gospel, or the gospel was absent altogether. I would have said that I was a Christian, but in fact I was lost. My main goal in life was to make a name for myself, whether it was in sports, professional advancement, or political success. So I became a lawyer and wound up in Washington, D.C., working for my home-state senator, the chairman of the Senate Foreign Relations Committee, in the hopes of making it big myself one day. I was where I wanted to be.

And yet when I got there, I was empty and unsatisfied. Being in Washington, the seat of national power, wasn't all that I had hoped it would be. I was lonely, disappointed, unfulfilled.

One day I went for a jog around Capitol Hill, where I lived. I ran past a building with a sign on it that read, Capitol Hill Baptist Church. I thought, *Maybe I'll go and make some connections or meet influential people.* I attended and began—for the first time ever—hearing the gospel clearly and powerfully preached. I didn't like it at first—what it said about God and what it said about me. But I continued coming along and I would shake the pastor's hand on the way out the door. He was Mark Dever, a friendly, outgoing fellow who would ask me to get together for lunch, which was the last thing I wanted to do. But one day, for some reason I picked up the phone and called him. We had lunch together and he sized me up immediately as a nominal Christian. He challenged me to get together with him at 8:00 a.m. on Wednesdays to study the Gospel of Mark. We worked through a six-session course called Christianity Explained, and the account of Jesus, his life and death, became clearer to me. At the same time I was observing the lives of the people of that church—they were different from me. They seemed to love one another genuinely and were not looking for personal gain or advantage, like I was. I came under increasing conviction that God was holy, that I was condemned, and that I needed to be saved.

One day I went home alone to my apartment after church and was reading John chapter 3 where Jesus says to Nicodemus, "I tell you the truth, no one can see the kingdom of God unless he is born again" (v. 3 NIV 1984). I realized then that I was a moral failure, that I couldn't turn over a new leaf but needed a new life. Then and there I repented of my sin and received Jesus as my personal Savior. "My chains fell off, my heart was free! I rose, went forth, and followed thee!"

For the next few years I was discipled in that church, found a faith-filled woman to marry, grew as a Christian, and eventually went to Southern Baptist Theological Seminary and returned to Capitol Hill Baptist to serve there as a pastor. For the last seven years I've been pastoring the United Christian Church of Dubai (in the United Arab Emirates), where we have seen many more people, including Muslims and Hindus, come to faith in Christ.

In the lives of those who appear on the fast-track, don't underestimate the power of the gospel.

9

THE UNDERESTIMATED GOD

J. Ligon Duncan III

Scripture quotations in this chapter are from ESV.

Many start out in Christian ministry thinking, *If I am faithful to God, if I do his bidding, if I trust in his grace, if I am empowered by his Spirit, I will not have the crushing darkness as a part of my experience.* Then it comes. Something happens and you are left asking God, "Why is this happening to me? What am I supposed to do with this? I did not think that it was going to be like this. At the outset of my walk with Christ, I did not see this coming. At the beginning of my ministry, I did not expect this." What is a Christian supposed to do in those situations? The Scripture teaches that God wants Christians to study their disappointments and to learn from them.

God wants us to study our disappointments, because if we look at our disappointments we will see what it is we love. When the bottom falls out, you will learn about what you love. You will learn things that you never knew before. You will learn what you really believe. You will learn where you really rest, where you really find your fulfillment and satisfaction and security. You will find what your real treasure is when the disappointments come. In every deep discouragement, in every deep disappointment, we are tempted to forget that God is God and that God is good. It does not matter how long you have been telling others that God is God and God is good, you are still vulnerable to not believing that yourself. The danger we face in disappointment and discouragement is that we are tempted to succumb to idolatry. Why? In times of disappointment and discouragement, we are tempted to think that there is a greater treasure that has been withheld from us. We are tempted to think that a greater treasure has been taken away from us, and that there is a greater treasure than what God has or can give to us.

This is illustrated in a study of God's dealings with Elijah in 1 Kings 19. In ministry, you do not want to find yourself in 1 Kings 19. You want to be in 1 Kings 18. First Kings 18 is where Elijah is God's instrument in the manifestation of his glory on Mount Carmel and the destruction of the false prophets of Baal. Or you may want to live in 1 Kings 21. That is the chapter that R. G. Lee of Bellevue Baptist Church based his famous sermon on, "Payday Someday." He preached it hundreds of times. The sermon begins with "I introduce you to Ahab, the vilest human toad to ever squat on the throne of Israel!" That is where you want to be in ministry.

However, we often find ourselves in 1 Kings 19, and it is a total shock. Also, the fact that chapter 19 follows 18 is a total textual shock. It is not what a reader expects. Before you go any further, take a couple of minutes to read those two chapters, and consider the heights of victory and the depths disappointment that God brought into Elijah's life.

I wonder, what are your greatest losses in life? What are your unfulfilled dreams, your unsatisfied desires, your plans, your yearnings, your longings? What are your hopes and treasures that you have never obtained, or that you have had taken away from you before your eyes. I do not ask whether you have had such losses—we all do. The question is, what will you do with them? How we respond may be the most important thing we do in life. Have you cried out deep in the darkness of the night through blinding, hopeless tears? Have you ever found yourself asking God, "Why?" and heard no answer. How have you responded to watching a life you have longed for slipping through your fingers right in front of your eyes? It is so hard to watch good and holy things slip through your fingers. Maybe you had such good things, and they were taken away. Maybe they have never been given. I wonder if you have felt like the Lord has brought you your greatest treasure, held it up before your eyes, and then closed his hand, saying, "You cannot have it." Maybe he brought it to you a second time, and then said, "You still cannot have it."

The story of Elijah is the story of a man of power. At this point in the Old Testament, no one except Moses himself had had this kind of ministry of power. Elijah yearned for good and great things, and he served the Lord courageously. He also knew what it was like to reach the end of his life with his hopes utterly dashed. He knew what it was to lose every dream. Yet Elijah can also testify to you of the ruthless, compassionate, pursuing grace of God in which he relentlessly goes after his ministers for his glory and for their everlasting joy. I want you to see that in 1 Kings 19.

The Lord Is God, Even in Our Disappointments

Even people who believe in God's sovereignty can fail to believe that the Lord is God, as we discover with Elijah. Elijah has just facilitated a spectacular display of the power of God on Mount Carmel. He has outrun a chariot, when a messenger arrives. The messenger has brought a message from the woman who has killed the prophets of the Lord in the northern kingdom, which essentially reads, "You think I am impressed by what you did yesterday? You think I am impressed by your killing of the prophets, my prophets, the prophets of Baal, the prophets of god, the god that I want Israel to worship? Well, by this time tomorrow, you will join them." Elijah's response to this is not what we expect. We expect Elijah to say, "Go back and tell her, 'Do you remember that fire that came from heaven yesterday?' You tell her, 'I will be right here! Ask her who exactly is it that she is bringing to me?'"

But this is not what he says. In 19:3 we are told that "he was afraid, and he arose and he ran for his life." It is tempting to ask, "What is going on Elijah? Have you just forgotten everything you've ever taught?" Elijah's name means, "My God is Lord." His name was a reminder that his God was Yahweh. That has been his whole message—"God is God! My God is God! The Lord is God! Your god is not! I serve the one, true, and living God!" Has Elijah forgotten that?

It is at this point where some of the modern commentators begin to psychoanalyze Elijah, and suggest that he is a manic depressive. He has all the classic symptoms. Yet these are ventures in missing the point of the text. Elijah is afraid; we are told that much. But I cannot see this as simply fear. This man has taken down hundreds of prophets of Baal and the king of Israel face-to-face just a day ago! This man is watching his world fall down around his ears. He is seeing his hopes dashed. This man is a disappointed man. This man is a discouraged man. This is not craven fear; this is a fear that his long-held dream will not be fulfilled. What does Elijah want? What is it that this man is living for? We see it in the text twice when God asks him what he is doing down in the wilderness. First in verse 10, and then in verse 14: "I have been very jealous for the LORD, the God of hosts. For the people of Israel have forsaken your covenant, thrown down your altars, and killed your prophets with the sword, and I, even I only am left, and they seek my life, to take it away." Twice he says it.

Elijah is telling you the truth here. He is telling you why his world has come crashing down, why the darkness has settled over him, why despondency has completely occupied him. He longed for that encounter on Mount Carmel to bring a nationwide revival in Israel wherein the Baals were thrown out and the one, true, and living God was worshiped. It is what he had lived for. He thought, *Lord, you are going to do it here in the fire! You are going to do it in a spectacular way. You are going to bring the godless house of Ahab down, thousands upon thousands across Israel are going to return to the Lord their God, and you are going to do it in a spectacular way.* In the very wake of this confidence, however, he gets a message saying, "You are going to be dead this time tomorrow." Elijah realizes it is not going to happen the way he has dreamed it would. What he has yearned for, what he is longing for, is not going to happen at all.

It would be easy for us to stand back and give spiritual counsel to Elijah right here. However, it would not resonate with him, because Elijah cares more about his message than most of us do, frankly. There is no way a man could be as discouraged as he is without really caring about the message that he is preaching. This man longs for God to be glorified. This man longs for God to be known as the only, true God, and when it does not materialize, his world almost comes to an end.

Maybe you are faithfully ministering to your church, and you long to see conversions and you are not seeing them the way you longed for. Or you are faithfully ministering in a church, and you see the false prophets around you, drawing in hundreds and thousands of souls, while you have sixty-five people, none of whom get along with one another. Or God has been so kind to bless your ministry with edification and with conversions, but your own son is a stranger to Christ. You have been crying out for twenty-five years for God to save him out of darkness, and he has not answered. Or you have been faithfully serving the Lord and you love Jesus and your wife loves Jesus, but you find yourself saying, "I did not know it was going to be like this, Lord. I just wish she liked me."

I do not know what it is for you—you fill in the blank. But the point is, there is discouragement that can come even to faithful servants. And when it comes, you learn what you love. You learn what you believe. You learn where you rest, where your satisfaction is, where your ultimate treasure is.

That is what is going on with Elijah. His deepest dream has been shattered, and so he runs. He starts running south, and he keeps running all the way into the wilderness.

Even People Who Fight against Idolatry Can Succumb to It

The second thing I want you to see is that even people who fight against idolatry can succumb to it. Elijah expresses his discouragement through fleeing in fear. The source of Elijah's discouragement was that he forgot the meaning of his name, and he forgot his message. This is a theological crisis, which is why psychoanalysis does not help us understand this passage. Elijah has suddenly forgotten what he has been preaching, and he has forgotten the God whom he wants Israel to embrace.

Once again, Elijah's name means, "My God is Lord." The Lord he is God!—that is his message, and he has forgotten it.

What does Elijah want? The answer is insinuated as Elijah sits waiting for God on Mount Horeb. First there is the whirlwind. It is an EF6 tornado. The mountain is dissolving. But God is not in it. Then there is the earthquake and the fire, but God is not in the earthquake, and God is not in the fire. Why the whirlwind, earthquake, and fire? They are pictures of what Elijah wants. Elijah wants

God to bring about revival in the northern kingdom by means of earthquake, wind, and fire. He wants a spectacular ending of the worship of the Baals, a spectacular declaration of God's lordship, a spectacular and nationwide embrace by men and women and boys and girls of God as the one true God. He wants a spectacular declaration that the Lord God of Israel is the only God and the one that they should worship. Yet it does not happen. God does not purpose to answer the cries of Elijah's heart with a spectacular "Yes!"

Instead, God is in the whisper.

This is confirmed, of course, by the errands on which God sends Elijah. God sends him back to Syria of all places. He says, "This is how this is going to go, Elijah. This is not going to happen the way that you have conceived it. This is going to happen through a Syrian—a pagan. This is going to happen through another king and this is going to happen not through you, not through your ministry, but through the ministry of another, Elisha." It is almost like Moses at the end of Deuteronomy. "Moses, I want to show you the Promised Land. Do you see it? Look at it good. You are not going in." When you hear a voice saying something like this in your ears, you can know it is probably the Lord God. He is the only one who works that way to bless his servants. If instead you hear a voice that says, "You really ought to have all you want. You ought to have it now," you can be assured that that voice comes with a hiss! However, when the Lord God draws near to his servants, he says, "You see it? You see what you've always wanted? It is good. It is good what you wanted. You cannot have it." When I hear that voice I say, "That is just like you, Lord. That is how you work."

One of the finest students I have ever taught in my twenty-five years had a son born with cystic fibrosis. At six years old, the boy said to his daddy, "Daddy, there's something wrong with me. Am I sick? Am I going to die?" And his daddy had to sit him down and say, "Son, you are not going to live as long as other boys. And son, you need to know that your father loves you, but I cannot help you here. I cannot do anything about it, but your Heavenly Father who loves you, is purposing this for your life. And your Savior, the Lord Jesus, only lived thirty-three years, and he did more than any human being that ever lived." He wrote me a letter about that conversation, and he said, "You know, my son shows a real love for the Word." The boy was seven years old by the time he wrote me the letter. "He is reading four chapters of the Bible a day"—seven years old and reading four chapters of the Bible a day! He went on to say, "I can see signs of responsiveness to the gospel in his heart."

Then came this in the last line of the letter: "Lig, I'd rather have him born again than well." As I read these words I said, "That is just like you, Lord. That is just how you deal with your most faithful servants. You ruthlessly crush their idolatry because of your compassion and grace for them and you want them to have a greater joy."

Our church is celebrating our 175th anniversary this year, and my mentor in historical theology at Covenant Theological Seminary, David Calhoun, was going to write our church history. A few years ago he had to write me a letter because his cancer had returned for the fourth time and the chemotherapy was destroying his heart. Now he was in congestive heart failure and dying from terminal cancer. He wrote me a letter to apologize for not being able to write the church history. He said, "You know, Lig, I said to my wife, Anne, it would be nice to have only one terminal illness, but the Lord, as always, knows best." I thought to myself, *That is just like you, Lord. That is how you deal with your most faithful servants. Not because you do not care about them, but because you do care about them. Not because you are not God, but because you are God. Not because you are not good, you are good. You do it because of your compassion and your grace. You wean their affections away from anything, everything other than yourself, and you leave them with nothing but you, nothing. Not their good desires, not their bad desires, not their good treasure, not their bad treasures, nothing but you.*

Elijah's message to Israel was to give up their idolatry and return to the one, living, and true God. God, in his kindness, refuses to allow Elijah to preach that message without believing it himself. Here is God ruthlessly pursuing his servant into the wilderness because he refuses to allow his servant's idolatry.

And is not the same true for you? He will not let you—you are his child, you are his faithful servant—he will not let you preach a message that you have not believed and experienced yourself.

You might say, "All Elijah wanted was revival! All he wanted was for God to be exalted!" But remember that Elijah had a way that he wanted it to be done, and it was not God's way. Do you understand that, when your Savior is in the garden sweating drops of blood and crying out, "My God! If possible, take this cup from me, nevertheless, not my will but yours be done," he too is fighting a battle against idolatry, and he is winning? "Not my will, but your will be done." God loves Elijah too much not to bring that message home to him.

Do you recall what happens next? God puts Elijah on the shelf. This is effectively the end of his ministry. Elijah does not finish well. Ian W. Provan's comments on 1 Kings 19:19 in the *ESV Study Bible* provide a succinct analysis of the situation:

> Is Elijah back on track as a result of his trip to Mount Horeb? The closing verses of chapter 19 suggest not. There is no mention here or in the upcoming chapters of Elijah's ever meeting or even trying to meet Hazael and Jehu. One never reads of Hazael's being anointed while it falls to Elisha to arrange the anointing of Jehu. Even Elijah's response to God's command about Elisha seems less than whole-hearted. There is no mention of his anointing

of Elisha as his prophetic successor. He merely
enlists him as his assistant.[1]

Elijah has all but had his day.

At this point you might be saying to yourself, "Lord, you are
hard. You are hard to your servants." When Elijah is in the wilderness, we are waiting for the Lord to draw near to him and say, "Be
encouraged, Elijah." But when the Lord sidles up close to Elijah in
the wilderness, what does he say? "What are you doing here, Elijah?"

I do not know what God's tone was in that moment. Did God
speak calmly and seriously, or was it a shout? I do not know how it
was said, but I do know that it is a rebuke. The Lord is not looking
for information. He is saying, "How did you get from there to here?
What does this have to do with your name, your message, your ministry? You've forgotten something."

Once again, you may think, "Lord, you are hard." But before
you settle on that conclusion, remember that in the wilderness when
Elijah cannot eat, God sends an angel to cook him a hot breakfast
and prod him into eating it (vv. 5–8). Remember that, when God
comes to him at the mountain of God, he comes to him purposely,
and he comes to him to display his glory to him. He says, "Elijah,
come out. Come out of the cave; come out of the mountain, because
I am going to display my glory." As far as we can tell, Elijah is so
despondent that he does not even come out when the whirlwind and
earthquake and fire are being manifested. He only comes out to the
still, small voice (vv. 12–13).

What does Elijah do? He wraps his cloak around his face. Now,
it is hard to see with a cloak wrapped around your face. God has said,
"Elijah, you are saying that what you have always wanted is to see my
glory. I am going to show you my glory." The scene is reminiscent
of Moses in Exodus 34. But surprisingly Elijah does not want to

see the glory of God. All he wants to do is die. Have you ever been there—that is all you want to do is die? Elijah is there.

God's Relentless and Ruthless Pursuit of His Servant's Joy

Then the Lord puts him on a shelf. This is it. This is the end of Elijah's ministry. He is sent on these errands in verse 15, and as far as we know he never goes. We do not see him again until 2 Kings 2. Take a moment to read verses 1–14 because there is a third thing I want you to see. Even when it looks like God is being hard on his servants, you can be assured that his provision is staggeringly and lavishly loving and generous and good and kind. And he will relentlessly and ruthlessly pursue you in his compassion, in his grace, for your joy. Let me direct your attention to verses 9 and 10:

> When they had crossed, Elijah said to Elisha, "Ask what I shall do for you, before I am taken from you." And Elisha said, "Please let there be a double portion of your spirit on me." And he said, "You have asked a hard thing; yet, if you see me as I am being taken from you, it shall be so for you, but if you do not see me, it shall not be so."

Elijah might be wondering, *What do you mean, "You want a double portion"? I've done more miracles than anybody since Moses. You want a double portion of that?* And what does Elijah mean when he says, "If you see me, you will; if you do not, you will not." The text then tells us what he means. Verse 11: "As they still went on and talked, behold, chariots of fire and horses of fire separated the two of them. And Elijah went up by a whirlwind into heaven."

Stop and consider: Do you not think that God knew the greatest desire of Elijah's heart? Do you think that God just leaves his soldiers on the battlefield? And do you think he does not care about *your* dashed hopes and *your* broken dreams?

With Elijah, a call goes out from heaven to the angelic host: "You go down and you go bring him home, and you bring him home by fire and whirlwind. I know my servant's heart. I know what he longed for. This is how we're bringing him home." Why does Elisha have to see that? Because he has to be able to give testimony to the inspired author of 2 Kings, "Let me tell you how God brought him home." Do you think that God does not care about the hearts of his servants?

It gets better than this. This is not the last time you see Elijah in the Bible. Elijah, we just saw, would not go out before the Lord and look on his glory. But one day a call comes from God, "Elijah, I want you to go down to a mountain again because there is something that I want you to see." In Luke 9:28–31 we read:

> Now about eight days after these sayings he took
> with him Peter and John and James and went up on
> the mountain to pray. And as he was praying, the
> appearance of his face was altered, and his clothing
> became dazzling white. And behold, two men were
> talking with him, Moses and Elijah, who appeared
> in glory and spoke of his departure, which he was
> about to accomplish at Jerusalem.

God speaks, "Elijah, go down. I want you to look into Someone's face." Do you know what Elijah saw? The light of the knowledge of the glory of God in the face of Jesus Christ—that is what Elijah sees on the Mountain of Transfiguration. God is saying, "My servant, I want you to look at something. You would not look at me on Mount Horeb, but I want you to look into the eyes of the Savior of the world, and I want it all to come clear." I imagine Elijah saying, "Lord, it was not enough that all of the northern kingdom would reject their idolatry and turn to the one, true, and living God. You wanted men and women and boys and girls from every tribe, tongue, people, and nation to see the light of your glory in the face of Jesus Christ. It all makes sense now."

That is how God works. He gets at our most fundamental idolatry, and he ruthlessly crushes it in his unfathomable love and fatherly kindness and inscrutable wisdom. He goes after our greatest treasures, and he leaves us with nothing but himself, so that we go limping on our way for the rest of our lives having learned, "My grace is sufficient for you, for my power is perfected in weakness."

Do not underestimate God. Do not underestimate his ruthless, compassionate, gracious commitment to his glory or his commitment to your everlasting joy and good. He will pursue you graciously and ruthlessly and rip out the idols of your soul that would otherwise consume you. He is working for your joy and your good even when you cannot perceive it and have ceased to be able to feel anything anymore.

I want to ask Elijah what the Lord said to him upon his return to glory after the Mount of Transfiguration, and I want to ask him what he said to the Lord, because there we see the Lord give him more than he could ask or think, even when he thought that the Lord had taken away everything that he had ever wanted. I just want to ask him, "What was that conversation like?"

That is the God you serve. That is the God we proclaim. Do not think that he will use you as his servant and then leave you to writhe in your disappointments. He has a plan for your everlasting joy in your declaration of the gospel that gives everlasting joy to everyone in the nations who by faith embrace him. Know that the Lord does not treat his servants' lives as cheap.

Your disappointments will be your greatest test. What you do in those moments means everything. Our response ought not to be the response of the disconsolate Elijah. We ought to say, "Lord God, this is what you built me for. This is what you have been doing all of my life. You have been leading up to this. You have been building me up to endure through this." That is why I think it is so wonderful that in the libretto of Mendelssohn's *Elijah* he has the words, "He that endures to the end shall be saved." Never was there a more appropriate theological application of a text to an Old Testament prophet's life.

NOTES

Introduction

1. Arnold Dallimore, *George Whitefield: The Life and Times of the Great Evangelist of the 18th Century Revival* (Carlisle, PA: Banner of Truth, 1970), 16.

2. Ibid., 15–16.

Chapter 1

1. One can find the T4G affirmations and denials at http://t4g.org/about/affirmations-and-denials-2.

2. "Affirmations and Denials." Please see thehe official website for Together for the Gospel at http://t4g.org/about/affirmations-and-denials-2 (accessed June 1, 2012).

3. Carl F. H. Henry, *A Plea for Evangelical Demonstration* (Grand Rapids: Baker House, 1971).

4. Charles Spurgeon, "The Whole Machinery of Salvation: Sermon #2327," preached August 18, 1889 in *Metropolitan Tabernacle Pulpit* (Pasadena, TX: Pilgrim Publications, 1975), 457–68.

5. Walter Ong, *Orality and Literacy: The Technologizing of the Word* (London: Methuen, 1982).

6. Duane Litfin, *Word Versus Deed: Resetting the Scales to a Biblical Balance* (Wheaton, IL: Crossway, 2012).

7. Lane Hall, *Works of Martin Luther with Introductions and Notes, Volume II* (Philadelphia: Holman Company and The Castle Press, 1915).

8. "One Race, One Gospel, One Task: Closing Statement of the World Congress on Evangelism," in *One Race, One Gospel, One Task: World Congress on Evangelism—Berlin 1966: Official Reference Volumes: Papers and Reports*, Volume 1, ed. Carl F. H. Henry and W. Stanley Mooneyham (Minneapolis: World Wide Publications, 1967), 6.

9. John Stott, "The Biblical Basis for Evangelism," in *Let the Earth Hear His Voice*, ed. J. D. Douglas (Minneapolis: World Wide Publications, 1975), 71.

10. Lausanne Movement. "The Lausanne Covenant." The official website for The Lausanne Movement is http://www.lausanne.org/en/documents/lausanne-covenant.html (accessed June 1, 2012).

11. Lausanne Movement. "The Cape Town Commitment" at http://www.lausanne.org/docs/CapeTownCommitment.pdf (accessed online June 1, 2012).

12. Christopher Wright, "According to the Scriptures: The Whole Gospel in Biblical Revelation" in *Evangelical Review of Theology*, ed. David Parker, vol. 33, no. 1, January 2009 (World Evangelical Alliance Theological Commission), 18.

13. "Go Tell It On the Mountain," lyrics by John W. Work Jr., 1872–1925.

Chapter 2

1. Richard V. Peace, *Conversion in the New Testament: Paul and the Twelve* (Grand Rapids: Eerdmans, 1999), 5.

Chapter 3

1. Spoken by George F. Pentecost at a missions conference in New York that took place April 21–May 1, 1900.

2. A. W. Tozer, *The Knowledge of the Holy* (New York: HarperSanFrancisco, 1961), 34.

3. Thomas Watson, *Farewell Sermons of Some of the Most Eminent of the Nonconformist Ministers* (London: Gale and Fenner, 1816), 220.

4. Richard Hofstadler, *America at 1750: A Social Portrait, Vintage International Vintage Series* (New York: Vintage, 1973), 240.

5. From "Crown Him with Many Crowns," text by Matthew Bridges.

6. George E. Ladd, *The Gospel of the Kingdom* (Grand Rapids: Wm. B. Eerdmans, 1990), 137.

7. Steve Corbett and Brian Fikkert, *When Helping Hurts* (Chicago: Moody Publishers, 2012), 27.

8. Dr. Josef Tson, "Thank You for the Beating," in the newsletter *To Every Tribe* (Fall 2009), 4–5.

9. Ibid., 8.

Chapter 4

1. This is a paraphrase of a line from J. C. Ryle, *Holiness: Its Nature, Hindrances, Difficulties, and Roots* (Moscow, ID: Charles Nolan, 2011), 69.

2. Calvin's Commentary on 2 Peter 1:5. *Calvin's Commentaries Volume XXII*, ed. John Owen (Grand Rapids: Baker Book House, 1993), 372.

3. Charles Hodge, *Systematic Theology* (Grand Rapids: Eerdmans, 1968), 3.215.

4. Herman Bavinck, *Reformed Dogmatics* (Grand Rapids: Baker, 2008), 4.253.

Chapter 5

1. Langston Hughes, "Salvation" from *The Big Sea* (1940) cited in James A. Haught, *2000 Years of Disbelief* (1996), 270.

2. Charles H. Spurgeon, *The Soul Winner* (New York: Cosimo, 2007), 28.

3. Charles H. Spurgeon, *Autobiography*, II.131.

4. James Hay and Henry Belfrage, *Memoir of the Reverend Alexender Waugh D.D.* (1839), 64–65 (cited in Sibbes, *Works* I.294).

5. Charles H. Spurgeon, *Lectures to My Students* (Grand Rapids: Zondervan, 1954), 12.

Chapter 6

1. Charles H. Spurgeon, *Lectures to My Students* (Grand Rapids: Zondervan, 1954), 154.

2. Ibid., 155.

3. Ibid.

4. Ibid., 165.

5. Ibid., 164.

6. D. A. Carson, *How Long O Lord?: Reflections on Suffering and Evil* (Grand Rapids: Baker Academic, 2006), 74, 81.

Chapter 7

1. Graeme Goldsworthy, *The Goldsworthy Trilogy* (London: Paternoster, 2001), 299.

2. C. S. Lewis, *The Last Battle* (New York: HarperCollins Children's Books, 1984), 228.

Chapter 9

1. Comments on 1 Kings 19:19, *ESV Study Bible* (Wheaton, IL: Crossway, 2008), 637.

SCRIPTURE INDEX